John Gibson

Agriculture in Wales

John Gibson

Agriculture in Wales

ISBN/EAN: 9783337327804

Printed in Europe, USA, Canada, Australia, Japan

Cover: Foto ©ninafisch / pixelio.de

More available books at **www.hansebooks.com**

AGRICULTURE

IN

WALES.

BY

J. GIBSON,

(Cambrian News.)

PRICE ONE SHILLING.

LONDON:
HODDER AND STOUGHTON, 27, PATERNOSTER ROW.
1879.

CONTENTS.

	PAGE
Preface	
Introduction	

CHAP.
I. Yearly Tenures and their Effects	1
II. Superstitions about Land	7
III. The Preservation and Reclamation of Land	13
IV. Land Proprietors	19
V. Garden and Dairy Products	24
VI. Fairs and Markets	29
VII. Hill Sheep and Escheators	34
VIII. Wool Growing and Management	41
IX. Servants and Hiring	46
X. Stock Rearing and Wheat Growing	52
XI. The Growth of Root Crops	58
XII. Cattle Breeding—Mongrels	63
XIII. Cattle Breeding—Pure Bred	68
XIV. Ground Game	73
XV. Planting—Wales a Land of Forests	80
XVI. Planting—The Revival of Arboriculture	86
XVII. Planting—The Future of Arboriculture	93
XVIII. Labour-Saving Machinery	98
XIX. Agricultural Societies	105
XX. Lime and Bones	111
XXI. Horses	118
XXII. Horses (Continued)	125
XXIII. Agricultural Education	131
XXIV. Sales by Auction	137

PREFACE.

My object has been to note the present condition of agriculture in the Principality, and to indicate, as far as possible, the directions in which improvements are needed. No attempt has been made to teach the farmer his business, or to lay down hard and fast rules of any kind. The scientific side of agriculture is beyond the writer's scope, and has not even been touched upon. There are certain well-known principles of business which must be observed by the farmer as well as by the tradesman, if he intends to succeed in his business. How these principles are neglected is pointed out in the following pages in plain language.

Farming is not in an advanced state in the Principality. The causes of this backwardness are touched upon, and, as far as possible, explained. There is, however, a growing desire for improvement, and attempts to point out shortcomings and to suggest remedies, even though the work may be imperfectly done, will be welcomed at least by those who desire to see the Principality take her place as one of the most carefully cultivated portions of the United Kingdom, although not by any means favoured with the richest of soils. During the past ten years a great improvement in the appearance of the country has been effected, and happily the spirit of progress is gathering strength and giving new signs of activity on every hand.

My thanks are due to agricultural friends in different parts of the country for numerous suggestions and much useful information. Indeed, some of the chapters could not have been written without the help of practical farmers acquainted with the actual work of cultivation. The substance of the work appeared in the columns of the *Cambrian News*, and is now published in this form after careful correction and revision.

Cambrian News Office,
 3, Queen's Road, Aberystwith,
  January, 1879.

INTRODUCTION.

THAT agriculture in Wales is in an unsatisfactory state will be admitted readily even by those who do not strongly believe in the possibility of effecting improvements except very gradually, and then only on the better sorts of land. The bulk of the land now under cultivation is high and poor. Here and there the rich soil of the valleys has been drained, but many of the low lands, for want of capital and enterprise, are undrained, and consequently of little use, except as occasional runs for cattle and sheep. The high lands, in many instances, are neither planted nor enclosed, and, consequently, return the owners low rentals, and afford the tenants no brighter prospect than a hard life, little, if any, better than that of a labourer.

In dealing with the agriculture of the Principality it is necessary to remember that there are many exceptions and limitations to every rule, and that what may be true of one district does not necessarily apply to another where apparently the conditions are the same. In Cardiganshire, for instance, there are landlords who plant liberally; in Merionethshire and other counties great drainage and reclamation schemes have been carried out; in the southern counties cultivation generally is more advanced than in the northern. In some parts attention has been given to sheep breeding; in others to black cattle and horses. Here the land is naturally more productive, or has been longer under liberal treatment; there it is subject to adverse climatic and other influences very local in their character. In short, it is impossible to write on a subject so varied without making great allowances, not only for varieties of soil and situation, but for differences in the cultivators, and in the circumstances under which they carry on their work.

Scattered over Wales there are good farmers who, with profitable results, cultivate the land according to sound modern principles. Landlords, too, can be found who give leases and recognize the right of tenants to the advantages accruing from the capital they have invested in the soil, and yearly tenants are not altogether unknown who farm with as much confidence as if they were freeholders. Notwithstanding individual cases of excellence, however, the average condition of agriculture is lower in Wales than in other parts of the United Kingdom; and, what is of more importance, lower than it need be, now that railways have opened up the country, and that education has been carried into the most remote districts.

For any honest attempt to point out ways in which the agriculture of the Principality needs improvement, or for suggestions as to how that improvement may be most easily and readily obtained, no apology whatever is required. Landlords who grant leases, who do not over preserve game, who maintain buildings and encourage improvements, may feel that due allowance is not made for them. Tenants, too, who struggle with great and numerous difficulties may smart under a sense that those difficulties are not recognized as they ought to be; but it must be recollected that the nature of a work of this kind necessarily involves that prominence should be given to defects, but it does not necessarily follow that excellences are ignored or under-estimated.

AGRICULTURE.

CHAPTER I.

YEARLY TENURES AND THEIR EFFECTS.

THE prevailing tenure in Wales is a yearly one, and, strangely enough, farmers themselves, in many instances, are not anxious that it should be superseded by leases. There is, indeed, a wide-spread reluctance to accept long leases, because they entail a considerable degree of responsibility to farm carefully, and almost certainly necessitate increased rents. This reluctance may probably be partly explained by the fact that a good deal of the land is exhausted, and cannot be restored to fertility without a large expenditure of capital, which, together with reasonable profits, cannot be recovered in twenty-one years—the longest lease granted in Wales. If the land were not so thoroughly worked out, a twenty-one years' lease might afford the cultivator ample time to reap the benefit of anything he put into it. The restoration of exhausted soil is work for owners or for capitalists who obtain long leases, and are protected by compensation clauses for unexhausted improvements.

Yearly tenants in Wales possess no security of any kind for the investment of capital in the land, and are averse to changes that would fasten upon them its restoration to fertility. The processes of exhaustion and dilapidation have been going on so long, that the farmer naturally shrinks from an undertaking which would entail an outlay equal, in many instances, to the present fee simple of his holding. If a lease is suggested to him, he looks round his farm, and what he sees is not always calculated to encourage him.

The sidelands may be fairly drained, but every flat place is wet and covered with water growths; the fences are fuller of gaps than quicks; gates are useless, and consequently absent; the house, unwisely built on the side of a hill, is neither weather-proof, comfortable, nor convenient; the farm buildings are more than half ruins, and if they were in good repair, are neither in the right place nor nearly large enough. The bad effects of a tenure that has failed in the past to maintain the productiveness of the soil are visible on all sides, and twenty-one years appears a short period in which to accomplish all that needs accomplishing, supposing he could have a fair start, a thing he knows is out of the question. The buildings, for instance, must be made the best of, and the drainage he cannot undertake to find capital for.

In old times there was, if not the feudal spirit, at least something akin to it, which gave tenantry confidence. Life was simpler then than now, and the absence of legal contracts was less seriously felt. Railways, education, and the numerous openings afforded by trade and commerce to men of enterprise, have not been without their ill effects upon agriculture. Slowly through the years farming in Wales has lost ground in the estimation of the people. It is no longer the favoured occupation to which men in the country apply all their energies, and with confidence put their eldest sons; but the last resource of younger children, who are too poor for business and too ignorant for the ministry. The lament that the old class of farmer—shrewd and intelligent—is dying out, is far from unfounded. He is, undoubtedly, becoming scarcer every year, and unless landowners insist upon leases and higher cultivation he will ultimately become extinct.

The improvement of an exhausted estate, although a slow and costly process, when compared with the improvement of a deteriorated tenantry is easy and cheap. The conditions under which agriculture is pursued in Wales are not now more unfavourable to the farmer than they were half a century ago. Both positively and relatively, the Welsh farmer is now in a better position than perhaps ever before. Markets are more numerous and more accessible; landlords are hampered by poverty, but they are disposed to listen to reason, and, according to their means, strive to make up for generations of past neglect; railways again have placed in the farmer's hands the power to produce that only which pays him—he is no longer compelled to grow on his own land everything he consumes, but may apply himself specially to that in which he obtains most success; emigration, too, by opening up new fields, in the colonies, has reduced competition for farms; whilst education has placed the liberal professions within reach of farmers' sons.

Landowners, called upon to make good the neglect of

their predecessors, are unable at once to meet the heavy demands for drainage, reconstruction, planting, &c., especially as the tenants are unwilling to pay increased rents for improvements, however indispensable those improvements may be. There are scores of estates in Wales that require the entire rental expended upon them for many years merely to bring them back again into fair cultivation; but instead of this, the rule among landlords, as well as tenants, is to take as much out of the land and to give as little back as possible. The landowner, for instance, whose estate will pass to a distant relation, looks carefully after expenditure, and, instead of improving the land, realises every shilling he can in order to make provision for daughters. What he is compelled to do by strictly worded covenants is all that need be expected from him, and that only grudgingly. Even when a landlord is willing to do what lies in his power to maintain in a state of efficiency, buildings, drainage, &c., on a large property, he is probably crippled by poverty, and cannot, without borrowing, invest the capital necessary to make his estate really profitable. That landlords, unable or unwilling to provide the capital required for the development of their property, should hesitate to adopt measures for attracting other people's capital, can only be accounted for on the presumption that landlords prefer decaying estates rather than the surrender of a little even of the appearance of the ownership of the soil.

The landowner, the bulk of whose estate is let on long leases, is as certain to become wealthier as the landowner who has nothing but yearly tenants to depend on is sure to become poorer. Not only will the land where leases are granted yield more produce, but the tenants themselves will improve with the soil. There are estates in Wales on which tenants are scarcely more in danger of eviction than if they were freeholders. In fact, the freeholder whose property is mortgaged may not only have to pay more rent, but be more in danger of being turned out than a yearly tenant. Cases could be given where freeholders have sold their farms to pay off mortgages, and have afterwards become tenants on those very farms at rents much below the amount they were previously paying in interest.

Small freeholders are probably the worst farmers in the Principality, and live from hand to mouth, a harder life than labourers. In no sense can their position be favourably compared with that of tenants on an estate where evictions are unknown, and where increased rents are seldom heard of. The great drawback of a yearly tenancy of this kind is that the farmer is able to live without much exertion, and is afraid to improve his holding lest he should bring upon himself additional rent. Although he is in no danger of eviction, and has but little to fear from revaluation, yet the remote possibility of a rise in his rent is sufficient to paralyze his effort, and to prevent him from manifesting signs of prosperity. How secure yearly tenants are on some estates may be inferred from the fact that the estates are virtually from intermarriages in the occupation of one family. These intermarriages go on from generation to generation, and owners of estates in Wales rather than rudely break up these clans put up with the losses and other inconveniencies of a low state of cultivation.

How far it is wise on the part of landowners to encourage a system that practically prevents the introduction of new blood and new systems is a many-sided question not easily settled. One thing is clear, that bad farmers keep each other in countenance, just as good ones stimulate each other to further efforts. In districts where a sort of clan has been established, and where old prejudices and habits effectually defy and bar out the spirit of reform, it may be necessary, when fitting opportunity occurs, to break in upon the circle by letting vacant farms to men from other parishes or districts, who are not imbued with the spirit of bad farming, and are likely to show a good example where it is most wanted.

CHAPTER II.

SUPERSTITIONS ABOUT LAND.

WELSH farmers are not less willing than Scotch and English farmers to make money, but they appear to be far less able to learn those lessons of thrift for which, at any rate, agriculturists in the more northern portion of the Kingdom are favourably known. The Welsh farmer is not extravagant in eating or drinking, and his clothing, of home made textures, is durable if nothing else. His daughters, who also wear homely stuffs, have not learnt boarding school "accomplishments," which give them notions above the farmyard, nor have his sons set up hunters, or taken to canes and eye-glasses.

Sir Thomas Phillips, thirty or forty years ago, gave a description of the Welsh Farmer, which, in many respects, still holds good. Brown bread of any sort is now scarce, and barley bread is unknown, but how truly the following extract describes many parts of Wales those know best who are intimately acquainted with the country:—"The Welsh farmer presents a stronger contrast than even the Welsh labourer to the same class in England. He occupies a small farm, employs an inconsiderable amount of capital, and is but little removed either in his mode of life, his laborious occupation, his dwelling, or his habits, from the day labourers by whom he is surrounded; feeding on brown bread, often made of barley, and partaking but seldom of animal food. The agricultural and pastoral population is for the most part scattered in lone dwellings, or found in small hamlets, in passes amongst the hills, or on the side of lofty mountains, or by the margin of a rugged sea-coast, or on lofty moors or table land, and oftentimes this population can only be approached along sheep tracks or bridle paths, by which these mountain solitudes are traversed."

Railways and improved roads, have done a good deal towards breaking in upon the isolation described by Sir Thomas Phillips, but many faults and deficiencies that still survive to vex the soul of the scientific cultivator are the remains of the old condition of things which is only slowly passing away, but which education will eventually kill. Agriculture in the Principality is hindered far more than is generally thought by superstitions and traditions which manifest surprising vitality, and are handed down from generation to generation almost unchanged. For instance, a field is said to have been cursed, and any attempt to drain and cultivate it is therefore not only deemed a going in the face of Providence, but is, of course, sure to end in loss and failure. There is scarcely a farm where there is not at least one "cursed" piece of land respecting which stories are told of disasters that attend attempts at cultivation. There is a field near Aberystwith —a meadow—known as "the fatal field." According to the legend, which is far more generally believed than well educated people are prepared to admit, when a sod of this field is turned an heir dies of the estate of which it is part.

With reference to bog lands there is a firmly-rooted notion that if they were drained the surface would dry into powder and be blown away. Another notion respecting bogs is that cultivation is out of the question unless the peat is cut or burned off, and as it is believed to be forty or sixty feet thick, this task is simply impossible —and, happily, unnecessary. This may be seen on the cultivated land round the edges of any undrained bog. Of course, if a few inches of turf can be ploughed into the clay, or if the surface peat can be turned into ashes, the processes of cultivation are greatly accelerated, but a bog only needs drains, lime, and cultivation to bring it into a fair state of tilth. In addition to the notion that the cultivation of bogs is impossible there is another held by those who admit the possibility, that the labour cannot be remunerative. Once break up the skin of the turbary, they say, and another will never form. Experience shows that when a bog has been drained the best course to adopt in order to kill the water growths and to create earth growths is to plough the land frequently, and by this means expose it freely to the action of the atmosphere. In Scotland, where possible, the peat is cut off and thrown into the rivers to be washed away. In other places good soil is carted upon the surface of the drained bogs.

That special places cannot be influenced by ordinary processes is commonly believed by numbers of men who would strongly repudiate an insinuation that they are superstitious. Not long ago we heard of a field which has the strange power of killing sheep if they are left on it more than a year! This peculiar field is also said to have an unbroken "pan" which defies the best plough, however strongly horsed. It is not difficult to see that a field with

a subsoil so stiff that it cannot be ploughed will be sour,
and will need draining. Farmers of the more thriftless
kind, always strongly inclined to superstitions, delight
in nothing so much as in showing fruitful portions of their
farms, which they say have received less liberal treatment
than other portions where the crops scarcely pay for seed
and labour. Suggestions that the barren land has only
been recently brought under cultivation, or that it has
been exhausted by a ruinous system of cropping, are
received with pitying smiles and assurances that the
barren and fertile lands are of precisely the same kind, and
have been dealt with in the same way for several generations. Sometimes the superiority of one portion of a farm
over another can be accounted for to the satisfaction
of everybody except those who are best pleased when
they imagine they have found a supernatural, or, at least,
very mysterious condition of things.

In discussions about the fertility of land nothing is
oftener heard in the Principality than that on this hill
side, or on that sheep walk, sheep and cattle will fatten
more quickly than on other lands, which, as far as can
be judged, are of the same soil. Not only does one farm
in Wales differ from another, but unenclosed and uncultivated land on the same farm varies greatly in its power
to produce nutritious grasses. The farmer, ignorant of the
past condition of the country, asks how this difference
is to be accounted for, and is so sure no answer can be
given that he does not wait for a reply. Let us see if there
is no answer. Apart from the indications given along the
sea shore, and in bogs, that Wales in ancient times was
covered with forests, there are laws, comparatively modern,
which show that down to a very recent date the hills of

Wales were covered with timber. In the fifteenth and sixteenth centuries laws were passed to enable "all the king's subjects and friends on horseback or on foot to pass freely through all or any of the forests of Wales." The forests of Wales four or five hundred years ago were dreaded by the Saxons who were compelled to travel through them, and the foresters of Wales were evidently a sufficiently numerous body to be legislated against. Without here entering into the interesting question how it happened that the forests of the Principality were destroyed, it is clear that those mountain sides which for a century or two were thickly covered with timber, would after the felling of the trees grow richer herbage than hill sides which had never been planted, or which were cleared two or three centuries earlier. This subject is referred to at greater length in the chapters on Arboriculture. Just as it is necessary to go back a century and a quarter, to the time when Montgomery landowners imported sires, in order to understand how it happens that the horses of that county are better than Cardigan horses, so it is necessary to go back still further to account for the superior pasture on one hill side over another. Where the land has been long under wood, it is, of course, richer than where it has been always naked. For the last century or two, however, there has been no timber growing, and the question naturally rises whether districts thickly planted in the time of Henry VIII. would still manifest indications of superiority over districts which at that time, and ever since, were bare mountain land. To say nothing of the protection from heavy rains afforded to the soil by timber, the yearly accretions of vegetation, and ultimately the decaying roots of the trees would be sufficient to give the sites of old plantations great advantage over open pieces of ground in the same locality. It will thus be seen that the superiority of one piece of land over another in Wales is not due to some awful and mysterious supernatural influence over which man can exercise no control, but to the very common-place fact that for a century or two the land was planted with trees, and was fed by the decaying vegetation of two centuries, and was at last left in possession of thousands of roots, which after loosening the earth were left to rot into manure. This is a common-place and a very prosaic explanation of a difference in the productiveness of soil, and those who feel desirous of clinging to more poetic but less reasonable explanations are at liberty to do so.

If Welsh farmers could once be persuaded that the soil may be deepened and permanently enriched by cultivation, and that agriculture is an honourable and might be made a profitable business, the Principality would not be long in taking a position more in accord with the boasted but not always obvious superiority of Welshmen over every other nationality.

CHAPTER III.

THE PRESERVATION AND RECLAMATION OF LAND.

SHORT rivers, wide estuaries, an extensive sea board, narrow valleys, fierce storms and sudden floods, make the preservation and reclamation of land two of the most interesting questions that can occupy the attention of Welsh landowners. During the past twenty or thirty years a good deal has been done by straightening and embanking rivers, towards protecting land and preventing further waste, but the wild uncultivated aspect of large portions of the Principality is due to the marsh-like appearance of the valleys, caused by the overflowing of rivers, which, in times of flood, spread over all the land to the bases of the hills. To add to the devastation, the detritus from the hills is carried down in large quantities and fills up the shallow beds of rivers, which are consequently driven into new courses. There is scarcely a river in Wales which, if left to itself, does not quickly convert good land into gravel beds. In some districts large sums of money have been expended in straightening and narrowing rivers, but how much necessary work still remains to be done in this direction may be seen on every hand. The preservation of land by embanking rivers is a very difficult task, not so much because of engineering obstacles, and these are neither few nor slight, as from the want of unanimity among the riparian owners. As soon as a river is narrowed it quickly deepens itself, and not seldom undermines and destroys the embankments made at great trouble and expense. A farm in Wales through which a river runs is not considered to be of more value on that account, but rather the opposite. A Welsh river is picturesque at all times, and when not polluted with lead, sparkles pleasantly as it eddies and dances over the rocks and boulders in its bed, but when the stream becomes a deep torrent, and the water flows with quiet gurgles through sedges, and creeps over grass lands, the farmer loses all sense of beauty, and feels that he has to deal with an enemy whose claims may not lightly be set aside. Pent between strong banks, straight deep rivers, like canals, are not as beautiful as winding streams that occasionally spread themselves over whole valleys, but they are safer and do not interfere with the cultivator of the soil. As a rule, rivers in Wales come tumbling down narrow gorges from their source in the mountains, and are allowed to meander unchecked according to the "lie" of the country down to the sea. All that is needed in many instances is that rivers should be straightened in order to enable them to cut out for themselves channels sufficiently deep to carry off the heavy floods which pour down from the high lands after heavy rains.

Tenants are deeply interested in this question, because floods subject them to considerable loss by washing away the land on the banks of rivers, and, in lead mining districts, by depositing on the vegetation injurious matter, in the shape of fine sand. A flood at the latter end of May or the beginning of June will destroy the hay crops, partly by "laying" the grass and partly by leaving upon it a coating of mud. It often happens that to keep a river within bounds the co-operation of a large number of owners at both sides is required, and without endless trouble cannot be obtained; but there are numerous instances where only three or four landlords are interested, and yet nothing is done in these cases. When a river has washed away the soil and left nothing but a bed of shingle, owners are apt to argue that the return on the capital required is too problematical to justify them in borrowing the necessary amount and making it a charge on the estate. In cases where whole fields are washed away, the damage is done so gradually that there is never any particular period when the owner feels that the demand for action is more than usually pressing. Besides, the labour of embanking a river is not infrequently thrown away. Rivers, as those who have had experience know, are not easily turned out of their old courses. Water is an insidious thing that finds out weak places in the best of work most unerringly. The number of acres of good land swept away every year by Welsh rivers is far larger than is imagined by those who have not carefully noted the decreasing proportions of fields adjoining rivers that flow with many windings through the land.

The greatest, or at any rate the most remunerative, reclamation of land could be made at the estuaries of rivers and the heads of shallow bays. All along the coast there are vast tracts of rich alluvial deposits which could easily be reclaimed and brought into profitable cultivation. Here and there something has been done with marked success, but far more has been left undone. The Dee is a well-known river, where land has been reclaimed. The Teify is another river where land may be reclaimed.

In many cases, which will recur to the minds of those acquainted with the Principality, the bases of the hills are washed by the tides at high water. The best of the land has been devoured by the sea, and, strange to say, next to nothing is done to reclaim it. It is difficult to estimate how many thousands of acres might be reclaimed in Cardigan Bay alone if the owners of land would join together and undertake the work.

When it is remembered how high lands are unfenced, under what great difficulties side lands are cultivated, and how level tracts in valleys are left undrained and at the mercy of rivers and the sea, the wonder is not that farmers and landlords are poor, but that they are able to live at all. Nearly every valley has its stream that at certain times becomes a torrent, and Welsh farmers know well what is meant when they hear that the "waters are out." Luckily the rivers are short, and as floods in Wales subside as rapidly as they rise, farmers are in some measure prepared for their enemy. There are indications all along the coast that the sea and the rivers combined have destroyed a great deal of land, a large portion of which might at any rate be reclaimed if landowners near the estuaries of rivers would either agree among themselves or allow capitalists to do the work without interference.

Much might be written about reclamation schemes

which have been more or less successful, but the object here is not so much to urge particular courses of action as to point out the nature and extent of the drawbacks and difficulties under which agriculture is now carried on in Wales. At the present time, Mr. Paddock, of Ynyshir, near Glandovey, is engaged in an attempt to reclaim from the estuary of the Dovey about eighty acres of foreshore, adjoining his own land. A tramway has been laid down, an embankment is in course of formation, and it is to be hoped for more than his own sake that Mr. Paddock's enterprise will be crowned with speedy and conspicuous success. Near Towyn in Merionethshire large tracts have been saved, and all has certainly not been done that might be done.

The land that might easily be saved from the Dovey cannot be of less extent than three or four thousand acres. There is, unfortunately, not much reason for expecting Welsh landlords, who neglect fencing, draining, &c., to take up the work of reclaiming land, but the work needs doing, and sooner or later the example set by Mr. Paddock and others will be followed on the Dovey and elsewhere. In the Aeron, Mawddach, Dee, and other valleys, sufficient has been done to prove that if in times gone by, land had been as valuable as it is now, the sea would not have been allowed to eat up the low lands, and yet to-day for want of sea walls, river embankments, drains, &c., land is allowed to become more and more the haunt of wild fowl and malaria.

The improvement of land by draining is making considerable headway in the Principality, but tenants are not willing to pay landlords five per cent. for draining, and, in the absence of long leases, cannot do the work themselves. Whenever a farm falls into the hands of capitalists draining is the first work undertaken, and it is almost incredible what a change is by this means effected in the much-abused land of Wales.

CHAPTER IV.

LAND PROPRIETORS.

IN the old times, when Wales was cut off from the rest of the United Kingdom far more completely than now, those owners of land who possessed houses on their estates seldom occupied them, and then only for very short periods. Before the advent of railways, indeed, the inducements to reside in Wales, it will easily be understood, were certainly not great, especially as the landowners rarely understood Welsh, and, when they appeared among their tenants, were besieged with requests hard to resist, for improvements calculated to make serious inroads on the small rents not over-regularly paid by the applicants. The tenants, few of whom could speak the English tongue, knew very little about advanced agriculture, and still less about their landlords. They were poor, laboured patiently and hopelessly under all sorts of disadvantages, and only indistinctly realised that their condition was the result of a system for which landlords might justly have been held responsible.

Railways, in addition to other benefits, have done a good deal towards making Welsh landowners less reluctant to reside on their estates, but the Principality still knows something of the evils that follow from non-resident landlords who let family mansions and the shooting to strangers, and leave all arrangements as to letting land, &c., to agents, who naturally enough stave off as long as possible outlay on repairs and improvements. Non-resident landlords are now the exception, however, and it is by no means unusual for the squire to take his natural place among his tenants, and, in many instances, to understand their language even if he does not venture to speak it. Without desiring to make too much of them, or to draw far-fetched conclusions from them, it may be mentioned that two important changes are going on in the Principality as regards the ownership of land. Merchants and successful professional men from over the border are beginning to compete for land in Wales, and whenever they come into possession the results are soon seen in planting, building, fencing, and draining. Again, in Wales itself successful business men in towns begin to turn their attention to agriculture. Freeholds up to a thousand acres are sought after at prices which tempt small impoverished owners into the market. When the successful townsman cannot purchase, he not seldom becomes the tenant of land on lease, and whether he makes money or not, soon effects improvements which make old-fashioned farmers shake their heads ominously and predict speedy ruin. The predicted ruin lingers long after the prophets are in their graves, and is still a coming event when a new generation confesses it sees nothing particular in the fields which once caused so much excitement in the neighbourhood. After it has been finally accomplished nothing is more difficult to realise than improvement in land. The value of land in some parts of Wales is very much higher than in England. In Cardiganshire, for instance, farms sell at prices which would astonish the inhabitants of Devonshire and other fertile portions of the country. The reasons for these high prices are that the land is in few hands and that the desire to obtain small holdings is very great both among the tenants and among Welshmen who have made money in England and desire to come back to their native country.

A word of explanation may be needed to account for the fact that leases are granted to shopkeepers or professional men more readily than to ordinary farmers. The reasons for this course are not far to seek. No landowner will grant a twenty-one years' lease to a tenant except at an increased rent. Now, the ordinary yearly tenant, as a rule, feels that he pays enough rent already and is anything but ready to pay more in order to secure a lease. He believes a lease is worth having if it can be obtained for nothing, but is too doubtful of the capacities of his holding to venture voluntarily upon the payment of additional rent. He will admit, perhaps, that his rent will be raised two or three times probably in the course of the next twenty years, but that does not seem to him a good reason for not avoiding the increase as long as possible. The shopkeeper or professional man acknowledges at once that to expect a long lease at the rent paid by a yearly tenant is unreasonable, and consequently offers to accept a five or ten per cent. rise in rent, on condition that a lease for twenty-one years is granted. This new class of tenant and freeholder is gradually displacing men who are just well enough off to live shabbily without working, but far too poor to maintain positions as county gentlemen. The new residents do not pretend to county grandeur, nor, on the other hand, do they fraternize with labourers, but are gradually forming a portion of what is known as the higher middle class, just the sort of people Wales has been most deficient in.

Poverty, pride, and pedigrees are no longer the distinguishing features of the bulk of Welsh landlords below the ten or a dozen great owners whose ancestors did not come over with the Conqueror for the simple reason that they were here before him. The gulf between the large owners of land and the people was wide and unbridged in the old times already referred to. The landlord took no part in public business, which was altogether conducted in a language he did not understand, and therefore did not like. The spread of education among the people, the decrease of prejudice against the Welsh language, and other causes, have brought the different sections of the people nearer together. Landlords are beginning to take an interest in Sanitary and Local Boards, and their influence for good is felt in many districts on Boards of Guardians and in all kinds of associations established for the advancement of the people intellectually and socially. The inhabitants generally speak a good deal of English, the landowners speak a little Welsh, and the relations between the classes are more friendly—or perhaps it would be more correct to say those relations are closer than they used to be. There are still, unfortunately, many drawbacks which prevent the growth of that higher middle class which has been absent from Wales in so marked a degree. Among those drawbacks must be placed the scarcity of good country houses, with from twenty to a hundred acres of land attached. A captain or major in the army, a retired lawyer or doctor, wants a place where he can keep a horse or two and dabble in experimental farming. He would gladly settle in Wales, but there is a remarkable scarcity of just the sort of rambling comfortable unpretentious residence—neither farmhouse, hall, nor mansion—which would suit him. Nothing is commoner than to hear that houses of this kind are wanted, and that some one has gone to live over the border because he could not get a place to suit him in Wales. The time has not yet come for Wales to be the fashionable rage, but every year a larger number of capitalists in England are discovering that the country is full of beautiful spots which only need the approval of royalty or some such stamp to bring them into notice. Two things are urgently needed, that landowners should invest capital in improving the land, and that they should give tenants the security afforded by long leases as an inducement to follow their example.

CHAPTER V.

DAIRY AND GARDEN PRODUCTS.

IN some parts of South Wales, and especially in great coal and iron producing neighbourhoods, farmers have been induced to pay more attention to dairy and garden produce than is paid in the less thickly populated portions of the Principality. In many districts the growth of vegetables is so neglected that they are brought in large hampers from England to the small country towns of Wales! The demand for eggs, fowls, ducks, fresh butter, fruit, and vegetables of all sorts is so pressing in the large towns of the South that it is not surprising some of these articles should be imported from England and elsewhere, but it is scarcely satisfactory that towns like Aberystwyth, Dolgelley, Portmadoc, Wrexham, Carnarvon, &c., should be compelled to go over the border for produce which Welsh farmers ought to supply in abundance, not only for local consumption, but for transmission to the English markets. The orchard in many parts of England is considered to be well deserving of care, but in Wales the growth of fruit is scarcely ever thought of by farmers except in isolated cases. Recently there have been indications that fruit-growing will receive more attention. Societies are springing up for the exhibition of fruit and vegetables and the smaller agricultural societies nearly always offer prizes for these kinds of produce.

If Welsh farmers, instead of putting butter down in salt, took it to the market towns they would soon find local customers, or dealers from a distance would take it away to the great centres of population. There is no good reason in these days of railways for salting butter and keeping it until it is worth twopence or threepence a pound less than if it had been sold fresh. In the old times, before railways were made, when butter had to be kept five or six months at the farm, and then sent a long slow journey in a cart, it was highly necessary to encourage the manufacture of salt butter, but now-a-days, when there are fast through trains to every part of the kingdom for perishable goods, it is of doubtful utility to give prices at agricultural shows for butter which would have fetched twopence or threepence a pound more without the salt. It is possible, no doubt, to say something on behalf of the old custom of salting butter, but that fact is not of much consequence. There are few bad customs respecting which something favourable may not be said; but these customs cease to be observed by sensible men when new ones are proved to be more advantageous. The shrewder agriculturists no longer make salt butter, but find a ready market for it at enhanced prices whilst fresh.

The average Welsh farmer is not a man who, accompanied by his wife or daughter, drives his cart into market every week, loaded with butter, eggs, fowls, vegetables, &c. He probably attends the fairs of the neighbourhood with some degree of regularity, but the butcher comes round to bargain with him for sheep and cattle, the egg collectors fetch the eggs he has to dispose of, and his garden produce as a rule is not worth mentioning.

Hens on ordinary Welsh farms are not well cared for. They roost in the cowhouse, probably, and pick up a precarious living as best they can. The garden, again, a piece of ground not well enough fenced to keep out the pig, is planted with potatoes in the spring, perhaps, but no attempt is made to grow fruit or winter vegetables. How much may be done with a garden towards making a small farm profitable is too well known to need recapitulation here, and it is very much to be regretted that in Wales gardens are not more highly estimated. In many parts of the Principality gardening is altogether neglected except by large landowners and labourers, to whom the towns are mainly indebted for constant supplies of fresh fruit and vegetables.

How it happens that poor Welsh farmers do not generally pay that attention to small sources of profit which are seldom neglected by the same class in other parts of the kingdom is a question well worth investigation. One of the chief reasons is that farmers in Wales do not employ a sufficient number of labourers to attend to the ordinary work on the land, especially when it is remembered that every ounce of turnip, hay, &c., has to be chopped by hand. So shorthanded are Welsh farms as a rule, that nothing can be done except ordinary routine work. Fences cannot be repaired, drains cannot be kept open, nor can roads be kept in order. There are generally, in fact, arrears of absolutely necessary work which cannot be overtaken, and consequently there is little prospect of the garden receiving careful cultivation. A water wheel, turbine, or windmill would enable a boy to do more work in an hour than two men can do in a day by hand, but water wheels require considerable capital, and windmills, although cheaper, are not as fashionable in Wales as in Norfolk and other parts of the United Kingdom. It would be hard to say how much money is wasted in Wales every year by the employment of men and horses to do work which wind or water would do far more effectively and cheaply.

Another reason why garden and dairy produce is not more in favour in Wales is that local markets are not as well-attended by dealers as they would be if farmers raised more produce and brought it regularly for sale. The dealer on one side, says he cannot visit a town for the sake of a couple of fowls, a score of eggs, or a dozen pounds of butter; the farmer on the other replies that it is useless for him to bring eggs, butter, cabbages, &c., to the market when he knows beforehand that he cannot sell them. All over the Principality there are towns where the markets are merely a name instead of being thronged every week by buyers and sellers. It is easier in London, Liverpool, Manchester, and other large towns to obtain fruit and vegetables than it is in Wales. Every year the Principality is visited by an increasing number of tourists, and one of their most constant complaints is that fruit and vegetables are scarce, and can only be obtained at very high prices. The failure of the Welsh farmer to turn his garden, dairy, and farm yard to the best possible account more certainly indicates his true position among agriculturists than more important shortcomings. A tenant may not be justified in draining a piece of land, or in grubbing-up old fences; he may not be able all at once to improve a breed of cattle, or to get rid of weedy horses; but there is nothing to prevent him from securing a good and profitable breed of fowls. If his cocks and hens are mongrels; if his garden fence is out of repair; and if his pig-sty is in ruins; he, and he alone, is to blame. His landlord may be a bad one, but he does not deserve a better. A farmer obviously careless about small matters clearly within his control cannot justly blame his landlord for treating him with suspicion and refusing to incur outlay which he has no reasonable ground for thinking will secure beneficial results. The only sense in which landlords are to blame—and in this respect they cannot certainly escape censure—is for not sternly insisting upon a better system of cultivation. A slovenly tenant has either been too long in one place or is altogether unfit for his position, and it is only fair to better men that he should be compelled to live a more thrifty if less easy-going life.

CHAPTER VI.

FAIRS AND MARKETS.

The ancient fairs, which in England have given place to weekly or fortnightly markets for stock and produce of all kinds, still flourish in Wales. Nominally, there are also market days, but except in large towns where there is great local demand for produce, strangers would scarcely distinguish any difference between market and other days. Here and there in the Principality markets which attract buyers from all parts of the country have been established, and have taken the place of all fairs, except, perhaps, a pleasure fair or two, associated from time immemorial with national holidays and festivals.

The absence of flourishing markets to some extent is supplied by middle men, who travel from farm to farm for the purpose of buying horses, cows, pigs, butter, eggs, fowls, &c. The hilly nature of the country has probably something to do with the difficulty of establishing weekly markets in Wales, but the reason given by farmers for not attending and supporting them is that the numerous fairs held in the course of the year meet all the requirements of the country.

The peculiarity of whole counties in Wales is that they possess no towns of considerable size. The million and a quarter of inhabitants are spread over twelve counties, and four hundred thousand of the people are found in Glamorganshire alone. Only three other counties have populations exceeding one hundred thousand, namely, Carmarthen, Carnarvon, and Denbigh. This population, sparsely scattered over the hills and valleys of the country, finds outlets for the produce of the land at the fairs held in every little town and village, and sometimes even on bleak commons, or at the junction of two or three valleys, apart from human habitations. Scarcely a week passes when there is not a fair within a radius of ten or a dozen miles from any given spot, to which the farmer carries or drives anything he has for sale. These fairs are attended by dealers who make this the chief part of their work. Recently, in some of the towns on lines of railway, monthly fairs for stock have been established, with varying degrees of success, but only seldom has the success been equal to that reached in England and Scotland. The absence of fat cattle in Wales materially reduces the chances of success in any attempt to establish weekly markets for the sale of stock and produce, but the fairs held in almost every village must be looked upon as the great obstacle.

The advantages of settled and well attended markets are greater and far more numerous than farmers have yet realized. There is in the first place the great advantage that results from attracting regular buyers from a distance, and inducing them to set up bases of supply. Traders in different kinds of farm produce settle in prosperous market towns and are not only always ready to buy, but willing to give the highest prices. Again, railway companies make special arrangements to suit buyers and sellers in good markets, and the commodities offered for sale at a Welsh town on Wednesday will be in some populous English centre early on Thursday morning. The agriculturists of a district are benefited by the prosperous market town in buying as well as in selling. Tradesmen find it to their advantage to provide farmers with seeds, implements, manures, &c., of better quality, and in greater variety than can be found in towns where markets are only a name.

The little village shop where everything can be obtained from a crochet hook to a plough, or from clover seed to Holloway's pills, is, of course, very convenient, but the pills may be as hard as peas and as dry as the clover seeds, which most likely would have grown better crops if sown five or six years ago. When there is not a quick and considerable demand it is impossible for tradesmen to keep large and well assorted stocks of seeds, manures, implements, &c., and yet without these the farmer's labour and capital are partly thrown away. It is natural to suppose that in towns favourably situated, shopkeepers alive to their own interests would unite and work together to establish markets. Strange to say scarcely anything is done by the inhabitants or public bodies of towns to encourage markets. Any expenditure on market accommodation is begrudged by the ratepayers, and any charge for tolls is evaded by farmers. Of course tradesmen will readily admit that it would be better for them if farmers came into town every week and obtained high prices for produce. They would obviously have more money to spend. The farmer on the other hand, if asked why he does not utilize his garden and make the most of his dairy produce, will in his turn ask what is the use of rearing fowls and making fresh butter if he has no market for them. In the great English centres of population there is room for all kinds of surplus produce if farmers and shopkeepers were only sufficiently enterprising to make it worth the while of dealers to attend weekly markets in Wales.

One of the first results of united action to establish markets in any district, say Bala, Machynlleth, Dolgelley Lampeter, or elsewhere, would be to decrease the number and popularity of fairs. Take a case in point. There are several fairs in the course of a year at a certain village. If the neighbouring town develops a market, these fairs, and others of the same kind, will be interfered with, but all the people of the villages where fairs were formerly held, will be benefitted by having near them a market where they find a ready sale for produce which could not be sold at the old-fashioned fairs. It must, of course, be admitted that good markets tend to reduce the number of places where fairs are held, but the fixity of markets and the greater accommodation provided far outweigh any possible loss in this direction. A prosperous market town is more advantageous to the farmers for twelve miles round than to anybody else, except perhaps the inhabitants of the town itself, and yet farmers and inhabitants rarely interest themselves in markets.

The farmer may work early and late, but his labour is unprofitable and useless unless he is able to command a market for his produce. This will be admitted by everybody when put in this direct, bald form; but to judge from the way farmers neglect markets, and even oppose them, it might be supposed that they were an invention for inflicting loss rather than gain upon the cultivators of the soil; or that they were a new experiment which, in all probability would end in failure and loss.

Great and immediate as are the advantages of good markets to farmers, it is not unreasonable to expect that the lead in establishing and improving them should be taken by the shopkeepers, who are also deeply interested in assisting farmers to obtain the best possible prices for everything they have to sell. If farmers are well to do, labourers will be in receipt of good wages, and tradesmen of every kind will share in the general prosperity. How little is done in most Welsh towns to encourage markets may be judged from the fact that public effort usually exhausts itself in the erection of a gloomy hall, which is partly market and mostly prison.

In many parts of Wales farmers' wives and daughters are expected to hawk dairy produce from house to house. This is partly due to old custom and to the absence of proper market accommodation. In these days when farmers' daughters are sent to ladies' schools, it is not likely that they will hawk eggs and vegetables from door to door, nor are they willing to come jogging to town in a mud-covered cart, or behind the servant man on a rough-coated cart horse.

CHAPTER VII.

HILL SHEEP AND ESCHEATORS.

HILL farmers devote themselves mainly to the rearing of sheep, and deserve far more attention and encouragement than they receive. Living far away among the hills, they make few claims upon public attention, except when an unintelligible boundary case has to be tried, or an equally unintelligible dispute arises as to the allotment of a mountain over which rights of common have been so long exercised that the land at last is claimed out and out by the adjacent freeholders.

In many parts of Wales hill farms have been greatly increased in value by being fenced, and in some cases planted so as to afford shelter, but by far the larger portion of the land is unfenced, and no inconsiderable extent of it is not allotted. Partly in consequence of the unfenced state of the farms, and the general backward condition of agriculture, together with the absence of lowland pastures and the neglect of root crops, the breed of sheep instead of being carefully attended to, was allowed to deteriorate year after year. Indeed, in some parts of Wales, Cardiganshire for instance, mountain sheep are said to be the least in the world. They can jump like greyhounds, run like hares, and get through nearly any fence that cannot stop a rabbit. Almost every farmer keeps a greater number of these sheep than his own land will maintain, and consequently they pass over the boundaries and are hunted back by adjoining tenants who are equally anxious to feed sheep on their neighbour's land. To still further complicate the relations of hill farmers, the boundaries, when marked at all, are seldom marked accurately, and are therefore continually shifting as the one farmer becomes more watchful, or the other more negligent. Improved mountain breeds are now obtaining more attention and at recent shows good judges say that great advances have been made, and that further improvements will follow the fencing of sheep walks.

The coursing of sheep, as the practice of driving them over the boundaries is called, is full of evil effects, some of which are obvious enough, but others, not less real and injurious, are not so easily traced. The custom is one of the results of not fencing mountain farms, but by no means the only one. Family feuds, handed down from generation to generation, break out every now and then, and are only kept within bounds by fear of the law.

The absence of shelter that fences would afford is in itself a loss of no slight magnitude, as may be understood by anyone who has watched sheep take refuge under trees, behind hedges, and in gravel pits. They always avail themselves of every scrap of cover they can find. It might be thought that this love of shelter would long ago have taught sheep farmers lessons that would save them large sums annually. Of course the work of fencing, if there were no questions as to ownership and boundaries, requires great capital, and should be undertaken jointly; but the addition to the yearly value of sheep walks, merely by fencing them, is so great that the outlay is soon returned. In some counties the work has been successfully accomplished to the great advantage both of owner and tenant. Besides all this, in many parts of Wales there is a class of people who reside in hilly districts; miners, blacksmiths, and others who, although they occupy very little land, if any, manage to keep from half a dozen to a score of sheep. These landless owners of flocks are a continual source of discomfort to the regular sheep-master who, although quite certain his animals are in the possession of his landless neighbour, cannot prove it. His marks may have been interfered with and others added until it is impossible to say whether the sheep were marked by design or by accident.

It is not difficult to understand that in a country where fences are the exception, and where the coursing of sheep is an established custom, estrays will be numerous. The characters of the escheators who take charge of all estrays, and the methods of escheating on different manors and lordships, are naturally of great interest to owners of flocks. The escheator, who is appointed by the Crown, is supposed to take charge of estrays, and to give notice in the parish church and in two market towns next adjoining the place where they are found, of the meetings held at regular intervals, when the farmers are called together to pick out the animals they recognise as former members of their flocks. In some districts the business of the escheator is fairly carried out, but in others there are strong complaints of the mysterious way sheep disappear, and the equally mysterious way escheators become well-to-do owners of small flocks. There are farmers who unhesitatingly denounce escheating as authorised sheep stealing, and doubtless the system, in the hands of men of dubious honesty may be made to tell with serious effect upon hill farmers.

Closely connected with the rights and wrongs of escheating, which are aggravated by the absence of fences, is that of sheep marks. In Wales, unfortunately, no register of marks is kept, and consequently from time to time disputes arise between parties anxious enough to do right, but unable to settle nice points respecting marks which are neither plain nor uniform. This confusion is strongly in favour of sheep stealers, who know equally well how to confuse a mark and how to swear it is their own. Of course, just as one dog that worries lambs is a nuisance to be got rid of from a district with all possible speed, so one purloiner of sheep may be a scourge in a wide neighbourhood to all honest men. Sheepmasters in Wales might with a little combination establish a registration of marks, and thus secure much greater freedom than they now possess from the objectionable practices of escheators and landless owners of flocks. It is to be regretted that sheep marking not only frequently fails in its first object—that of enabling owners to identify their animals—but is often accompanied by a good deal of unnecessary cruelty. The animals' ears, for instance, are sometimes split in a way that can only be justified by the erroneous assumption that sheep are as fond of having their ears slit as it is said foxes are of being followed by a pack of hounds! Nothing so conveniently disposes of arguments against cruelty as confident assurances that the animals enjoy that which is called torture by simple people.

Among sheep farmers in Wales there is one practice, not it is to be hoped extensively followed, of shearing lambs in autumn, and thus depriving them of their natural and very necessary protection against the severe weather of winter. Lambs shorn before they are about eighteen months old are rendered much more liable to contract diseases than if left in their wool, and, it is scarcely necessary to say, the farmer loses more by disease and death than he gains by the wool. The reason given by farmers for shearing lambs in autumn is not without some show of reason. It is better, they say, because of the heavy rains for lambs to be shorn in autumn than to carry a lot of wool through the winter. The lambs if heavily woolled, it is contended, never have time to dry thoroughly, and suffer more from wet than from the consequences of clipping. Lambs, yeaned in March probably, are clipped at the latter end of September, and even as late as the end of October, but the sheep are clipped in June or July. If the lambs are shorn in autumn they must go through the winter with three or four months' growth of wool upon them less than is carried by the sheep, but if left unshorn they carry extra wool, and there can be little doubt they need the protection it affords. Lambs yeaned in January and February might be clipped in July without cruelty. The evils caused to unshorn lambs by heavy winter rains ought to be met by fencing the walks and providing shelter, and not by clipping them late in the autumn. This is not the place to enter into a discussion as to the choice between two evils, but it is equally clear that lamb-clipping in autumn is cruel and unprofitable, and that the nature of the climate on the hills calls loudly for fences and shelter.

There is a tendency, which agricultural societies would do well to encourage, to replace the small Welsh mountain sheep by larger breeds from Scotland. Unfortunately the prizes offered at some shows are not for the best mountain sheep, but for the best Welsh mountain sheep, which are too small to be profitable. Sometimes it happens that an enterprizing farmer imports larger sheep, and instead of doing well they die mainly from continued exposure. Not only is he discouraged, by this but others who hear of the disaster are led to believe that nothing will do for the Welsh hills but the small native breed. In Breconshire and Radnorshire the hill sheep are larger and more profitable than in Cardiganshire, and some other counties.

Success in breeding and feeding sheep depends largely upon the cultivation of root crops, which are neglected in many parts of Wales far more than they ought to be. In districts well adapted for turnips these roots are not nearly so generally grown as wheat, which frequently costs more to grow than it fetches in the market. Without suitable shelter, pastures, and winter feed it is impossible for sheep to do more than keep themselves alive on high lands.

In connection with sheep farming in Wales it is pleasant to note one great improvement, due mainly to

Mr. Ellis, of Bala, who has been the means of successfully establishing sheep-dog trials in the country. These trials are very interesting as spectacles, and fortunately one of their effects has been to induce agricultural societies to give prizes for the best sheep-dogs. The more hill farmers can be induced to take interest in their important business, and to study how to improve it, the sooner will landowners see the wisdom of fencing their lands so that they may be brought into better and more profitable cultivation.

CHAPTER VIII.

WOOL GROWING AND MANAGEMENT.

Wool is a valuable part of a hill-farmer's produce, and everything pertaining to its growth and preparation for the market is therefore of importance to him, and deserves to be carefully noted. Welsh fleeces in good condition are amongst the finest in the world, but they are often unequal in quality. The wool, too, is frequently greatly reduced in value by the presence of kemp, by dirt, and by the unequalness in the quality of the fleece. The wool from the neck and shoulders, as a rule, is very much finer than that about the hips and tail. Kemp, or rough white hair, is due to poor feeding, and the low condition of the animal. Want of proper nourishment and the absence of shelter, together with the fact that mountain sheep are coursed persistently from one walk to another are sufficient, without taking into consideration defects in breeding, to account for the presence of kemp which greatly reduces the market value of the fleece.

When kempy wool is put into the hands of workmen to be dressed the dry white hair drops through the machines, and, of course, is lost to the manufacturer. Sheep having once begun to grow kemp there is danger that they will bear lambs whose wool ultimately will be more or less mixed with it, however well they may be fed, or however carefully they may be shepherded. The difference in the fineness of the wool on the fore and hind quarters always exists, but it becomes more and more marked as sheep are neglected and insufficiently fed.

The loss to which sheep masters are subjected by kemp and unequal fleeces might be considerably reduced if careful choice were made of rams well and uniformly woolled, and if sheep were regularly and sufficiently fed all the year round. It is doubtful, however, in the absence of fences, root crops, shelter, and good hay, whether sheep masters can possibly do justice to their flocks, which, if well fed, would be far less liable than at present to ticks, other vermin, and disease.

It may reasonably be urged that tenants cannot be expected to provide fences, and that all the evils arising out of unfenced sheep walks should in fairness be laid upon landlords. A flock master cannot erect sheds on an unfenced sheep walk, for instance. There is something in this, but for another great defect in Welsh wool—its uncleanness—the tenant himself is altogether responsible. Want of cleanness is an inexcusable fault, and one that costs the farmer more than he can well afford. Dirty wool does not readily find a market, and fetches a less price than clean sorts. Dealers and brokers in Liverpool and elsewhere know what it is to have on their hands large quantities of Welsh wool which does not find buyers simply because it is not as clean as Colonial clips.

In Wales, too, stored away in barns, bedrooms, and

all sorts of unlikely places, wool may be found which would have been sold long ago at the prices for which it is held back if more care had been taken in washing and shearing. As a rule so little care is taken to secure the fleeces in good condition that they far too often bear the colour and substance of the ground on which the sheep were pastured. The farmer's first care ought to be to grow wool of good quality, but his next concern should clearly be to secure the fleeces in the best possible condition. It would be unreasonable, perhaps, to expect Welsh sheep farmers to rival Australian colonists in the management of wool, but all that can be done by labour and carefulness ought to be done.

In some parts of the colonies sheep farmers first of all construct a large wooden bath, capable of containing from one to two thousand gallons. A lye composed of two pounds of soda and one pound of soap to a hundred gallons of water is prepared, at a temperature of 110°. In this bath a dozen or more sheep are made to swim at once for five or six minutes. The animals are then driven up an inclined plane and allowed to drip for a time. They are then placed under a douche of cold water, poured down from a fall of six or eight feet. Two men hold each sheep, which is turned about until its whole body has been subjected to the cold stream. The newly cleansed animal, with its wool white and clean, is then turned into an enclosure, where it remains a few days before the clipping commences. As many as two hundred thousand sheep are passed through this process in one season on single Australian farms, and by it the dirtiest fleeces are thoroughly cleansed and increased in value.

Welsh sheep, to begin with, are, as a rule, very insufficiently washed, and instead of being clipped in a field are raced over dunghills, and allowed to trample among the mire of the farmyard, or are penned in a house with a filthy floor, and clipped where cleanliness is almost impossible of attainment. Farmyards, stables, cowhouses, barns, &c., are not fit places in which sheep-shearing should be carried on by farmers anxious to make the most of their wool. There are in Wales sheep masters who carefully wash and clip their sheep, but a good deal is lost by that inattention to good methods which seems to run through the farmer's business life. Just as sheep are clipped in houses and barns, the wool is stored in sleeping apartments, and kept year after year waiting for a price that, if at last obtained, does not yield as much profit as if the clip had been sold before rats and other vermin got possession of it.

Something might be said about the unhealthiness of storing wool in dwelling-houses, but it is perfectly hopeless at present to persuade rural populations that all sickness and death are not works of Providence which ought not to be interfered with.

The work of sheep-shearing is one that requires a steady, skilful hand, and no one except a regular shepherd should ever be allowed to handle the wool-shears. The damage done by wounding sheep with the shears is far more extensive than is supposed. Inflammation sets in and death often ensues. The fleeces again are easily damaged by the shears when placed in the hands of inexperienced men. In some parts of Wales the whole work of wool management is exceedingly rough and unbusinesslike. It is almost incredible that there are sheep masters who seldom or never count their flocks, so that losses from careless shearing and other causes are not found out as they would be if the sheep were counted at stated periods. Fleeces should not be marked with pitch, which is insoluble, but with Archangel tar, which is a little dearer, but preferable. Raddle and other mineral substances should only be used sparingly and when absolutely necessary.

The farmer may say that some of the defects here pointed out, admitting their existence, only affect the manufacturer, and that the farmer obtains as much for his wool now as he would if greater care were taken to get rid of kemp and dirt, and to send fleeces into the market as white and pure as wool is supposed to be, and as Colonial wool had at first to be in order to obtain a market in this country. Very likely there are some advantages in dirt and idleness, but it is generally admitted, whatever they may be, that they are not equal to those arising from cleanliness and industry. This is true of most departments of life, and Welsh farming is no exception to the rule.

During dull times like the present Welsh fleeces are almost unsaleable, although Colonial wools meet with a comparatively ready demand. With ordinary care it is in the power of farmers to make Welsh fleeces the best and most marketable in the world. But to do this lamb-shearing, as practised in some parts of Wales, must be abandoned; sheep must be dipped to kill vermin, and so put an end to rubbing; pitch must be abandoned as a marker; greater care must be exercised in washing; the shearing must be done by experienced men; and more than all, perhaps, sheep-walks must be fenced, and sheep-coursing must be entirely abandoned.

CHAPTER IX.

SERVANTS AND HIRING.

IT will be readily admitted that without servants carefully trained to all kinds of farm work agriculture cannot possibly make rapid advances. Skilled agricultural labourers are scarce in Wales, and hitherto, unfortunately, their work has not been done by machinery to anything like the same extent as is the case in other parts of the United Kingdom. The higher class of farm labourer is not in much demand, and as he finds liberal remuneration in the quarries and lead mines of the North, and in the iron works and coal mines of the South, he seldom turns to the land for a living except in times of trade depression, old age, or after he is weary of the more exhaustive but better paid forms of labour.

The miner or quarryman when business falls off or health declines, finds his way back to the farmer and resumes the employment of his youth, but he is not a skilled labourer who takes pride in his work, and in many respects has not been improved by his experience as a quarryman or miner. He has gained a knowledge of the world, which inclines him to look with contempt upon the farmer and his occupation, and he has lost the simple pride he once possessed in straight furrows and well-tended horses. Large numbers of labourers on the land have at some period of their lives worked in the quarries of the North or the mines of the South, and farmers know to their cost that rumours of a new quarry or mine are calculated to rob them of the most promising of their young servants.

Owing to quarries, lead and coal mines, iron works, and a steady flow of emigrants to America and the Colonies, the wages of agricultural labourers are higher in Wales than in many parts of England, where the land is much richer and labourers are more skilful and harder worked. Welsh emigration has never reached anything like the proportions it attained in Ireland, but there is a steady flow of the better sort of farm labourers and small farmers to America and the Colonies. Besides the Welsh settlement in Patagonia there are colonies of Welshmen in America who contrive to support Welsh newspapers and to establish places of worship where services are conducted in the old, well-beloved language.

At home the difference between the farmer and the labourer is seldom one of breeding or culture, nor are employer and employed far removed from each other socially. If the labourer is married he may occupy a small mud cottage and live a hard life enough, but if single he lives and is lodged as well as the farmer, and of the two has more money to spend. He seldom saves anything, scarcely ever thinks of joining a friendly society, and deems it the duty of the ratepayers to maintain his parents without assistance from him.

The existing system of changing from place to place and of going to work away from the land, together with that love of poetry and music which prevails among the working population, have resulted in labourers being more intelligent and better educated than ordinary tenant farmers who have lived all their lives on the small farms they occupy, and have only heard of the places and scenes their servants speak of from personal knowledge.

The farmer is borne down between rabbits and undrained land, but the labourer gives his spare time to poetry and literature, and is enabled by these studies to take a prominent position in the village church or chapel choir, and to contest for prizes under some high-sounding bardic name at eisteddfodau. His verses may be very lame and inconclusive, and his prose rough to ruggedness, but his compositions, however worthless, elevate him into the possession of a genuine if narrow appreciation for literature not found elsewhere in the United Kingdom among the same class of men. Not long ago at an eisteddfod held in a mountain village in Cardiganshire, twelve sets of eight men each contended for a small money prize for singing a piece of music. These ninety-six competitors went through the piece in a way that showed that they had at least an intelligent conception of the spirit of the composition, and some of these sets of eight manifested a skill that told of long practice and patient labour.

There is of course another side of the farm labourer's life. To begin with, he is engaged at a hiring fair. No questions are asked about his character or antecedents, and as long as he does his work and abstains from poaching, he is not troubled with much interference from his employer or his employer's landlord. His sleeping apartment is not, perhaps, in the farm-house, but wherever it is he is under no obligation to go to bed at any given time.

Farm labourers are apt to ramble about in the night time from one farm-house to another, and the custom of the country allows female servants to admit the men to the farm-houses. There have been many fierce contentions as to the degree of immorality that prevails in Wales compared with other parts of the country. That the surroundings of farm-servants' lives are conducive to immorality cannot be questioned, and that the results are not more serious must in part be attributed to the familiarity of the people with conditions which if less common would be more likely to rouse the passions. It has been proved that bastardy is not more common in Wales than in England, but it is notoriously true that in the rural districts a large number of women are pregnant before they are married. On the other side, it should be stated that prostitution is not known in Wales to anything like the extent it is known in England. The home life of the poor is not favourable to purity, and every well-wisher of the people must long to see better houses erected.

The relations between farmers and labourers, begun at hiring fairs and terminated after a year's service, cannot be expected to include any of those mutual obligations which naturally grow up between employers and employed when the master is something more than a payer of wages and the servant is not a mere seller of physical force to be employed at the will of the purchaser. There are numerous instances in Wales where labourers are as well cared for as the same class in other parts of the kingdom, but no general improvement can be expected in the condition of the working population until farmers themselves are more prosperous, and pay more attention to intellectual culture and social comfort.

Female labour is an important feature in farm work throughout large districts of Wales. Women work in fields, tend to cattle, work in the harvests, &c.; in short, work on the land just as men do. The 'morwyn benna' (head woman) is exempt from field labour, except, perhaps, during hay and corn harvests, but the rest labour in the fields like men. The annual hiring fairs are crowded with women—hard-handed and coarse-featured—engaged without characters by farmers who are not supposed to take any interest in, or exercise the least care over, the servants in their employment, beyond seeing that they attend chapel or church on Sunday.

Far oftener than ought to be the case, servant men either sleep in the same room with the women, or pass through the women's apartment night and morning. It is not an easy matter to say how the evils due to small and inefficient farm houses are to be remedied, but as a sense of impropriety is awakened, women will refuse to go to service at farms where the sleeping arrangements render privacy and decency impossible. The engagement at hiring fairs is not calculated to deepen a women's self respect. She stands there to be bargained for like any other animal, with the exception that no questions are asked as to whether she is vicious, good-tempered, &c., questions always asked in the case of a horse. The modest, well-behaved girl is no better off than the impudent and forward. All that is wanted is a field hand who will not be over particular either about work, food, or domestic arrangements. There is no occasion to draw a highly-coloured picture of the life of a female agricultural labourer. She must obviously hear much that a woman ought not to hear, and be subjected to much that a woman ought not to be subjected to.

Machinery would be cheaper than women, who then could easily find more congenial employment in domestic service, especially if they were better acquainted with the English language. As regards hiring fairs, it is impossible to say anything in their favour. From first to last they are full of consequences thoughtful men must contemplate with pain. Registry offices, private hirings, and monthly engagements might do much to mitigate the evils of these fairs, but the first thing needed is a deep conviction in the minds of farmers that the hiring fair is a degrading institution fraught with all manner of evil to servants, and consequently not beneficial to farmers. If farmers, as often as possible, engaged servants continuously, subject to a month's notice from either side, hiring fairs would soon fall into disuse, especially if servants were allowed holidays at convenient seasons to make up for the week or fortnight now wasted in leaving old places and settling down in new ones. The wages of male servants are equal to about twenty shillings a week—the actual remuneration being board and lodging and from £25 to £30 a year. Women, in addition to board and lodging, are paid from £8 to £15. What farmers require is greater skill in labourers, and to secure this it will be necessary to introduce labour-saving machinery more extensively, and to take greater interest in farm work themselves.

CHAPTER X.

STOCK REARING AND WHEAT GROWING.

UNSATISFACTORY as the conditions may be under which hill farmers pursue their business, and that they are unsatisfactory nobody will deny, yet hill farmers have certainly less reason to complain than the cultivators of side land farms. Never perhaps since "Hu the Mighty first showed the method of ploughing to the nation of the Cymry, when they were in the country of the summer before their coming into the Isle of Britain," was the ordinary farmer so hardly pressed on every hand as now. The sheep breeder on the hills is sure of ready markets and high prices for his mutton; but the grower of wheat and the rearer of cattle finds himself face to face with foreign competitors, who have made wheat growing a losing business, and now send beef across the Atlantic to markets once thought safe from this kind of intrusion.

The cultivation of wheat is still pursued in many parts of the Principality, and, when the seasons are exceptionally favourable, the crop may not result in actual loss. There can be no doubt, however, that wheat crops should be abandoned for oats, barley, turnips, mangolds, and other feeding stuffs for cattle. This is the opinion of the best judges, who at every agricultural meeting speak of the uselessness of growing wheat in a moist climate, and the folly of neglecting root crops.

Unfortunately there are two erroneous notions that cannot be got rid of except very slowly. The first is that farmers ought, as far as possible, to grow on their own land articles required for home consumption, although they may be able to obtain some of them at much less cost and of better quality in the nearest market town. The second is that cattle cannot be fattened on ordinary Welsh farms, except at great loss, and that, therefore, it is necessary to sell store stock and to purchase fat cattle in England. In many parts of Wales, even twenty years ago, it was inconvenient, if not impossible, for farmers to obtain many commodities required in their own households except by growing them. In those days wheat was grown not only for home consumption, but for sale. The crop, it is true, failed now and then, but the demand for home-grown wheat was constant owing to the cost of transit and the great uncertainty of foreign supplies. Unfortunately for the home wheat grower, there is now not only no uncertainty as to foreign supplies, but the construction of railways, the introduction of steamers, and the improvement of roads, have placed the Principality more nearly on an equality with the rest of the United Kingdom than ever before in her history. The only possible excuses for growing wheat in Wales now depend on covenants and on the mistaken notion that good farmers should grow wheat whether the land and climate are adapted for it or not. The climate in Wales is far too moist for wheat, which only makes a good crop when the seasons are so dry that nearly everything else fails. In what are known as the grain-growing districts of England the breadth of land devoted to wheat has been considerably narrowed, but in Wales not only do many farmers still grow this crop as heretofore, but follow with great fidelity the antiquated methods of harvesting it which prevailed in the times of their grandfathers.

Great as the loss undoubtedly is of growing wheat on side-land farms in Wales, there is some show of reason for the custom. In a country where money is scarce it is not surprising that the inhabitants should hesitate to part with it to purchase breadstuffs which their fathers certainly grew at a profit. The reluctance to fatten stock for which there was no home market was intelligible enough before railways were made, and when stores had to be driven long distances. Although there is no further reason for that reluctance, yet the influence of old custom still makes itself felt. There is now no difficulty in disposing of fat stock, which ought to be more profitable to farmers than stores. The notion that animals can never be fattened on Welsh farms it will be seen on examination rests on no foundation more substantial than imagination and experience based on unfair trials. To start with, the average tenant farmer is so badly off for buildings and other shelter that he is not in a position to undertake the fattening of the stock he rears with any reasonable chance of success. Professor Tanner, in his *First Principles of Agriculture*, recently published, says:—
"Some few years since it was very common for the

stock kept through the winter months to lose nearly all the flesh they had gained in the preceding summer, simply because sufficient food was not supplied to prevent the waste of the body. It is now known to be not only cruel but unprofitable, and such bad management is, in consequence, rarely seen at the present day," except, the Professor might have added, in Wales. Without convenient farm buildings and shelter it is impossible to fatten cattle in Wales or elsewhere in the United Kingdom. In Scotland and England nutritious grasses are carefully grown, root crops are extensively cultivated, and cattle feeds are studied and used. If these aids are necessary in Scotland and England, it is out of all reason to expect that in Wales cattle can grow fat on moss, rushes, and east winds. The hay grown in Wales is not, as a rule, overpoweringly rich but no pains are spared to remove from it in the course of harvesting any nourishing qualities it might at one time have possessed.

In addition to defective buildings, impoverished pastures, poor hay, and other drawbacks, the Welsh tenant farmer is not provided with the necessary machinery and power to enable him to cut up food for fattening stock. When buildings are large and comfortable, and when the farmer avails himself of the means used over the border for fattening stock, he succeeds in utilizing the frames he rears and of course secures the profit which is often lost because Welsh land is considered to be incapable of feeding cattle.

Notwithstanding the importation of American beef, the rearing and fattening of stock will undoubtedly

be the most profitable part of a farmer's business for
many years to come. The rearing of frames for
English graziers to cover with flesh is a most unprofitable and thankless labour, and yet this is the
work that Wales does for the English farmers, who
are perfectly willing to encourage the idea that time
spent in feeding cattle in the Principality would be
lost. With warmth and plenty of suitable food cattle
will make flesh in Wales as well as in Scotland. Of
this there can be no doubt. If Scotland can supply
London and other centres with fat beasts, surely Wales,
with a better climate, could do so too if Welshmen
paid that attention to breed and feed which is paid
to them in the north. Put nothing in the land
and you cannot expect to get much out; but the
land is faithful, and if much is put into it nothing
will be kept back.

It would not be difficult to mention farms in every
part of Wales where the tenants or owners fatten
stock; but the rule is to sell stores for other people to
fatten. There is, however, a sufficient sprinkling of good
farms and intelligent farmers in the Principality to
prove that the country only requires men of capital
and enterprize, possessed of secure tenure and free from
the liability of increased rents, to increase its productiveness far beyond anything of which there is promise
at present. The landlord looks at his thriftless tenant
and, naturally enough, hesitates to force upon him a
lease he does not want. The tenant on his part knows
his landlord is too good-natured to turn him out
and yet has not sufficient confidence in him to
manifest signs of great improvement lest he should be

asked for increased rent. The cause of bad farming in Wales it cannot be too often pointed out is not so much dread of eviction as the fear of increased rent. If landlords made long leases the rule they would soon find their farms assuming a more prosperous appearance. Tenants that are not deserving of leases are clearly not deserving of farms, and ought to be got rid of. The decay of buildings and the general ruinous appearance of so many holdings is due to yearly tenancies, which in the long run are far more injurious to the landlord than to the tenant. The tenant may, at any rate, send his children into business, but the landlord must retain his exhausted land and ultimately expend capital in rebuilding ruined houses and buildings.

CHAPTER XI.

THE GROWTH OF ROOT CROPS.

UNTIL farmers in Wales recognize far more vividly than at present the advantages of growing root crops, it is hopeless to expect any great change for the better in their condition. Without turnips and mangolds it is simply impossible to fatten stock, and one important question for every farmer to consider is whether land in the Principality is of such a nature as to make roots a profitable crop. There can be no doubt that Wales owing to its moist climate is admirably adapted for roots. This, happily, is abundantly proved in different parts of the Principality by farmers who, clearly understanding the nature of their business, carefully prepare the land for this indispensable crop, and make arrangements for consuming it on the most advantageous terms with a view of converting it into beef and mutton.

The farmer who refuses to grow roots does not openly venture to say his land is not suitable for them, but shields himself under the assertion that feeding stock does not pay, and consequently growing root crops must be an unprofitable undertaking. It is almost impossible to contend successfully against a general assertion of this kind. The fact that only respectable well-to-do farmers feed stock is urged on one side to prove that feeding can only be undertaken in Wales by "fancy" farmers, whilst on the other the contention is that they are well-to-do because they feed cattle, and thus reap the fruits of their labour. This is received with cynical incredulity.

The old rule in Wales was to sell off stock in October when grass began to fail. Thirty years ago, when white crops were more popular in England than they are now, farmers from over the border came in autumn to purchase stores in order to utilize straw, &c., grown by them under agreement. The methods of cropping in England have greatly changed, and the demand for cattle in autumn has fallen off, whilst the spring demand has greatly increased. Notwithstanding this change, however, many farmers in Wales still persist in keeping stock through the summer to be sold in autumn for £2 a head less than could have been obtained in spring, in addition to the loss of five months' keep. Some of the shrewder sort of Welsh farmers purchase store stock from their neighbours in spring and autumn and feed them at great profit. If cattle must be sold as stores they ought to be parted with in spring when they are two years old, and not in autumn when they are eighteen months, nor yet a year later when they are two years and a half.

For the reasons already explained prices in autumn do not rule as high as in spring, and therefore farmers ought to be in a position to keep cattle through the winter and bring them into the market in May when the demand is often far greater than the supply, and prices are favourable to the seller. Of course, hitherto it has been taken for granted that Welsh farmers must sell nothing but store stock, but this is not by any means the case. There is no reason why most of the animals should not be sent out of Wales ready for the butcher, if farmers generally gave to cattle feeding that attention which is given to it here and there by individuals who do not by any means possess special advantages.

Seeing that roots are indispensable to the farmer who undertakes the fattening of cattle it cannot be out of place briefly to canvass the reasons why in Wales this crop is not more popular, especially as it is generally admitted the soil and climate are well adapted for them. To begin with, land intended for swedes or mangolds should be sufficiently well fenced to secure it from the intrusion of sheep and cattle. This preliminary condition is well known to every farmer, but unfortunately thousands of them are utterly unable to comply with it. To put down five or six acres of turnips every year would entail considerable expense in fencing. Apart from turnips good fences would be advantageous if they would not convey to landlords such an idea of prosperity that the tenant's rent would, he fears, be raised just in proportion to the sum he seemed to have at his disposal for fences and the indulgence of "new fangled notions about fattening cattle which his father sold as stores." One of the first consequences of growing root crops would be that appearance of order and prosperity which the yearly tenant dreads more than anything lest it should induce his landlord to demand more rent. This dread of increased rent paralyzes the yearly tenant at every turn, and especially when considering the advisability of adopting methods of cultivation which it is well known entails some reserve of capital, however small. He firmly believes that nothing enables him to keep down his rent at its present figure but the maintenance of a conviction in his landlord's mind that he is absolutely too poor to pay more. How remarkably Welsh farmers succeed in this object is well known, nor can the fact that they frequently train their sons for the learned professions be taken as proof that they hoard money, because in the Principality very poor people make great sacrifices in order to train their sons for the ministry. Not unfrequently when a young man in Wales has failed as a farmer, and perhaps also in some other business, he betakes himself to the ministry, the only profession in the Principality in which it is said there are no failures.

Besides the difficulty of fences, there is the much greater one of the expense entailed by the preparation of the land for root crops. The average farmer has neither the labourers nor the horses to prepare the land for swedes or mangolds as it should be prepared. Whilst he is ploughing and cleaning five or six acres for roots everything else is at a standstill. Of course just when he is wanted on the land he is most urgently required in the buildings to chop food for his animals, and as everything on the farm must be done with the least possible assistance, he is always trying, with poor success, to catch the tail end of the seasons.

When his opportunity is clearly lost he consoles himself with the reflection that next year he will succeed where he has failed this. At last the seed is sown in land more or less carefully prepared, and afterwards the crop is spoiled for want of cleaning, or deteriorated for want of sufficient thinning. Turnips require space in order that they may grow, but when the plants are small the temptation to leave them too thick in the ground is great indeed.

From first to last the green crop tests the farmer very severely at every step. His thoroughness is put to the proof in the preparation of the land; his cleanliness and punctuality by the way he attends to the young plants; and his business capacity by the way he harvests and uses his crop. In many districts the neglect of cattle feeding is so great as to be the rule, and throughout Wales it may with safety be said that root crops are not cultivated as they ought to be.

CHAPTER XII.

CATTLE BREEDING—MONGRELS.

WELSH black cattle are well known all over the United Kingdom as hardy animals which have not yet been "improved" into barrenness and into a condition of tenderness useless for everything except stall-feeding. Pure-bred Welsh animals are able to hold their own in the English markets, and command excellent prices wherever they are offered for sale. Whether the Anglesey and Castle Martin strains are two distinct breeds or are offshots of the same parent stock are questions that specialists may be left to argue and decide as best they may. Most likely a good deal that is interesting might be be said on both sides, but no good purpose would be served by entering into the discussion here.

The immediate object of these lines is to note the actual condition of cattle breeding and rearing in the Principality, and to point out excellencies and defects, without, on the one hand, entering into controversial subjects, or, on the other, professing to teach practical farmers their business. The rage for Shorthorns, of course, spread into Wales, and at agricultural shows held in different parts of the Principality splendid specimens of this famous breed are frequently

shown. The same may be said of Herefords, and of
other less popular sorts.

The friendly rivalry among landowners, which followed
the introduction of agricultural societies and the establishment of annual shows has already resulted in a
marked growth of interest in cattle breeding, and it may
reasonably be hoped is destined to influence for good
even the most wilful propagators of mongrels. Formerly
attention was almost exclusively devoted to Shorthorns,
but recently the wisdom of studying the merits of the
native black cattle has been recognised in high quarters.
It is no longer a sign of bad taste, and Welsh "national"
exclusiveness, to breed black cattle even to the utter ex-
clusion of those showier kinds which are not so well
adapted to the country. Welsh pastures, it is well
known, are far from rich, except where the land has
been improved. On average farms in Wales cattle require sound constitutions to enable them to live through
the winter without losing all the flesh made in summer.
In winter Welsh stock is inured to great changes of
temperature and accustomed to pick up a scant living
on hungry land. When taken into rich lime and bone-
dressed English pastures, and supplied with roots and
cake, they put on flesh with such astonishing rapidity
that they are always in good demand among dealers
who know their good points.

The Welsh cattle trade with England is not a thing
of yesterday. An agricultural return of about a hundred
years ago states that in Anglesey there were at that
time large herds of cattle—a hardy race much sought
after by English dealers, who, it seems, bought the cattle
on credit and did not pay for them until after they

returned into Wales from the English markets. We read that the poor farmers of Anglesey suffered considerable loss by this system, as the dealers often professed not to have realised good prices, and sometimes never returned at all. That such a system could prevail speaks well for the average honesty of the dealers and shows that in the old times Welshmen were of a confiding nature. Anglesey is still noted for its cattle, but dealers do not now obtain long credit. Several times it has been pointed out that in writing about agriculture in Wales no general rule can be laid down which is not subject to numerous exceptions. This is particularly true respecting cattle breeding. It may be asserted, for instance, that Welsh farmers ought to breed black cattle, but in a country so diversified as the Principality there are numerous valleys where Shorthorns, Herefords, Ayrshires, and other sorts will flourish as successfully as in England. On an improved farm, well sheltered and fenced, and adequately provided with outbuildings, root crops, and machinery, cattle that would starve to death on an impoverished holding, may be reared with profit.

Notwithstanding the exceptions that must be made for soils and situations suitable for other than Welsh black cattle, and where, therefore, no reason exists for adhering to the native breed; notwithstanding, too, the other and still larger class of exceptions in North and South Wales where pure-bred black cattle have superseded other sorts and are rapidly growing in favour, there is still a wide and undisputed field for improvement. Many popular customs are justly open to adverse criticism, and although no suggestion, however wise, can possibly be of universal application, much might certainly be done even by the smallest of tenant farmers, and on the poorest of land, towards breeding and feeding cattle on principles calculated to make profits larger and more certain.

There is good reason why tenant farmers who cultivate the ground under a yearly taking should not spend money in drains, bones, fences, gates, &c., but there is no reason why they should not buy pure-bred cows and secure pure-bred sires. The first cost of pure-bred black cattle is not very much more than that of mongrels, whilst the loss through having mongrels is not only great, but continuous. Mongrel cattle, with Welsh black for a basis, eat as much as if they were pure-bred, and perhaps more, but their stock when brought into the market are not able to command high prices. Half-a-crown or five shillings saved in a sire, and fifteen shillings or a pound saved in cow will entail a loss of from £5 to £8 a head when the motley herd, all colours, sizes, and ages, is brought into the market. In some parts of Wales, Cardiganshire for instance, the neglect in the choice of sires for horned stock is very great indeed. In fact, it may be said, that in that direction no care at all is exercised. Each farmer keeps at least one mongrel bull of his own, and his stock consequently degenerates. At every fair in the county referred to, it will be seen that there is one bull for every three or four cows. The idea of paying for a well-formed pedigree sire is altogether out of the question, and in the absence of good pure-bred dams, this negligence is not much to be wondered at.

Again, instead of timing their cows to calve in March

or April, as is the custom among good farmers in several parts of the Principality, no rule is practised, and young stock on a farm are therefore not even of uniform age. Where attention is paid to the breed of cows and careful choice is made of sires, the calving will be timed for the spring of the year, and the results are young stock of uniform breed, colour, age, and quality. No great keenness is required, to see that a lot of two-year-olds of this description will more quickly attract buyers and obtain far higher prices than an equal number of animals varying from two to three years of age, and of every possible mixture of breed and colour. English dealers come down and buy these mongrels in great numbers, and afterwards sort them out into more even lots. A herd of two-year-old mongrels will sell at from £7 10s. to £8 10s. a head, whilst pure bred animals of the same age, uniform in colour and quality, will fetch from £13 to £16 a head. The difference in these prices represents the profits which a fore-handed farmer makes, but which are altogether lost by one who pays no regard to cows, keeps mongrel bulls, and is not mindful to secure all his calves in March or April. There is no department, perhaps, in which a poor man can so easily compete with his richer neighbours as in the excellence of cattle, apart, of course, from fancy breeds. The Welsh black eats no more when pure bred than when thrice mixed, and is worth a fourth less money. The sum of five or ten shillings may have been saved by obtaining a mongrel bull, but it is quite as likely that the crosses were obtained by allowing a mongrel, kept at great cost, to run with the herd.

CHAPTER XIII.

CATTLE BREEDING—PURE BREEDS.

THE results of permitting unselected stock to interbreed year after year cannot, of course, be satisfactory. Trouble, in the first instance, is saved, but poverty is encouraged, and, unfortunately, a fine animal is occasionally produced and shown all over the neighbourhood in support of the belief that good stock is not reserved to those who spend money freely. The evil consequences of in-breeding, however, where no choice is made of dams or sires, are too well known to need recapitulation here: weak points are exaggerated until they become deformities, and equality is utterly lost. When animals are pure bred, sound, and of good form, in-breeding within reasonable limits may sometimes be advantageous, but the practice is one that ought rarely to be followed except by breeders possessed of good judgment and of great experience, who know what points they desire to see brought out prominently. In this as in other matters mediocrity should be content to travel in the ruts.

The natural effect of in-breeding is to transmit the defects and excellencies of parents in a stronger and more marked degree to the offspring. The even balance that should characterise a good herd of cattle is upset, and the farmer suffers loss when he brings his motley, unequal stock into market. In-breeding, deliberately adopted to obtain certain results, is one thing, but in-breeding, which is the result of ignorance and carelessness, is another and altogether different thing. It is scarcely credible that in some parts of Wales farmers are so careless that any sort of male is allowed to become the founder of a herd, and that no care whatever is exercised to keep up a regular supply of fresh blood. Ill-formed animals—notorious mongrels—are allowed to repeat with exaggeration their own defects in generation after generation of progeny until at last it is almost impossible to say whether the base is Hereford, Black, Shorthorn, or something else not recognized by breeders, and not admitted into herd books.

Graziers from the Midland Counties who buy stores in all parts of the United Kingdom say that they find the worst kind of cattle in North Cardiganshire. The lower end of the county and the district further south are more favourably known. In North Wales, too, there are saleable animals, especially of the Welsh breed. At the last Royal Show the Black Cattle class was highly creditable to the Principality, and it may be stated with confidence that even in North Cardiganshire there is a marked improvement in the horned stock, although much still remains to be done.

Landlords at comparatively light expense might do a great deal towards improving the breed of cattle by keeping pure-bred bulls for the use of their tenants at nominal fees. Landlords in Wales have not yet done all that may reasonably be expected of them towards improving the breeds of animals of different kinds. On a large estate the cost of keeping a pure-bred bull or two for the use of tenants would scarcely be felt, and although farmers at first might not appreciate the advantages offered to them, they would do so ultimately. If landlords did something towards helping their tenants in this respect they might speak with force against the habit of rearing males which cannot do a worse thing for farmers than leave stock behind them. It is to be feared that as long as tenant farmers rear mongrel bulls pure-breds will have no chance, simply because of the trouble entailed by a journey of a mile or two. It is so easy not to take trouble, and as the carelessness is sanctioned by the custom of many generations it is not likely that for some time to come mongrel bulls will be the rare exception that unerringly points out the slovenly farmer who lives from hand to mouth, and attributes his want of success to providence or ill-luck.

There are landlords who take pride in the prosperity of their tenants, but there are also landlords who are not sorry to see the gulf between owners and cultivators of the soil kept wide and deep by any means. The squire who feels he is neither very rich nor very highly educated tacitly encourages, or at any rate sanctions, slovenly habits and ruinous customs which he would strongly oppose if he were surer of his own position. A prosperous farmer on three hundred acres of fair land might easily run a poor squirelet a very hard race in many unpleasant ways.

In laying the foundation of a breeding stock, one object may be to raise a herd the best of its kind,

This work requires money; and, as whoever undertakes it should be independent of profit, the tenant farmer is excluded. In the majority of cases, however, the object in laying the foundation of a breeding stock is to raise cattle for the market with the greatest possible margin of profit. This is the legitimate business of the ordinary producer, and if pursued intelligently, backed by knowledge and capital, is as safe and profitable as any other business, with this advantage, that the producer cannot easily overstock the market. Notwithstanding the recent development of the meat trade between America and the Colonies and this country, the most profitable part of a farmer's business for many years to come in Wales will be the rearing and fattening of stock. This fact it is necessary should be impressed upon the farmer's mind.

The producer must have a model in his mind such as he desires to reach. His cows must be carefully selected, and the male must have a long and pure pedigree. The cows that throw the best calves should be retained, whilst those that "cry back" should be dismissed, and their places filled up with new selections. By careful selection for a few years a profitable breeding stock may be established by the average farmer, without any unreasonable expenditure of money. Of course he ought to attend yearly pedigree bull sales in the spring of the year, and when he secures a first class animal, money ought not to tempt him to part with it. A good deal of experience will be required to teach the average Welsh farmer that the best thing he can do with a good animal is to keep it, unless he is offered a fancy price beyond its market value.

If there were no other reason for obtaining pure breds than the difficulty of fattening mongrels, that ought to be sufficient. Sour-visaged steery-looking cows are far too common even in districts where a better class of animal is not difficult to find, and no great change for the better will be effected until the farmers resolve only to breed from bulls of pure breed, whose stock is well known for its excellence. If rents were fixed, as only long leases could fix them, farmers would not be afraid of possessing herds of pure-bred cattle, and there would then be no temptation to assume that appearance of poverty already alluded to, merely to persuade the landlord that additional rent would end in ruin to the tenant.

Those who remember the country ten years ago will readily admit that during that short time great improvement has been effected in the breed of cattle, and there can be little doubt that farmers are now more alive than ever to the necessity for care in selecting breeding stock. One of the greatest hindrances to advancement is the deeply-rooted notion that bad farming is more profitable than good farming; and that the herd of mongrels though it sells for less money is more profitable than the same number of pure-bred animals. This impression will not easily be got rid of until education has got a firmer hold than at present of the agricultural population; and until the cultivation of the soil is looked upon by young men of capital as an honourable business in which skill and assiduity are sure to be fairly rewarded.

CHAPTER XIV.

GROUND GAME.

THE mere mention of ground game is unhappily more than sufficient to cause landlords and tenants to become alike unreasonable. A farmer eaten out by rabbits is not in a fit state of mind to listen patiently to fine distinctions and theories. It may be true that if owners of land could not get shooting at home they would go abroad for it, and that other remote evils might have to be faced if those arising from game were got rid of as completely as most farmers would get rid of them. The farmer's answer to this is that he will prepare to meet distant evils if he can be relieved from the plague of rabbits, which are an ever-present unmitigated curse, in his opinion only to be effectually removed by extermination.

Apart from what they eat—and the amount is by no means inconsiderable—the farmer dreads rabbits more than blight, or drought, or flood: these he is at liberty to fight against, and not seldom rising markets enable him to look with complacency on what at first seemed like unmixed evil. But rabbits have no redeeming feature. They bring leanness and barrenness to the tenant who is compelled to feed them and, perfection of wrong, to pay a good round sum per acre for the ruinous privilege.

If he does not complain about this modern and very effective method of levying black-mail upon him, it is because he does not wish to be put down for a discontented, grumbling fellow, who is always airing his grievances. Experience has taught him that grumbling yearly tenants either find their way to smaller and poorer farms, or get removed off the estate altogether. Tenants who believe it is good policy not to grumble are not likely to sue landlords for damages, except in very extreme cases, or when they have made up their minds that they would improve their position if forced to seek a fresh farm.

Actions for damages done by rabbits prove nothing as to the amount of injury done to crops every year, and afford no adequate indication of the wide and deep feeling of discontent in the minds of the farmers against landlords who preserve these destructive rodents.

Rabbits have been denounced with a persistent vehemence that leaves their enemies nothing to desire; but still they multiply until farms change hands quickly or stand empty because of them; they are carefully preserved by landowners, many of whom are little more than wholesale game dealers, and often a good deal less, in that they feed game on land for which high rents are paid by poor tenants who are often compelled to suffer in silence.

Sport is one thing, and feeding rabbits for sale at the expense of tenants is another and very different thing. Now-a-days the landlord accompanied by a few of his friends, does not walk over the ground gun in hand, as was the custom twenty or thirty years ago, picking up a moderate bag by the end of a hard day's work. Then the farmer hailed the sportsman with delight and gladly pointed out a covey, a brace of long tails, or a hare. Now the game is nursed and watched. A day is fixed and the victims are carefully gathered together for slaughter. The "potters" surround the game which is to be murdered wholesale and packed off at once in hampers to market. Three or four of these big days may result in heavy returns of killed, but the sport is nowhere. The farmer is as unable to see the fun of the killing, enjoyed by his master, as to understand the reasonableness of the feeding, *not* enjoyed by him.

Aristocratic rabbit merchants and game dealers who own large estates are not more tolerable than their brethren in trade, who, on considerably less than a thousand pounds a year, try to live as if they had five or six.

Rabbits reared on tenants' land bring in these needy squires a good round sum which seems to be all profit. That they are in the long run as unprofitable to the landlord as the tenant is, however, not difficult of proof. Rabbit-infested farms deteriorate steadily in value, and if rents do not actually decline they fail to keep pace with land where this pest is not encouraged. Nor is the decline in rental by any means the only ill effect of vermin-breeding as far as landlords are concerned. The tenants themselves deteriorate. Doomed to work land poisoned and burnt by rabbits, farmers lose heart and cease at last to carry on a struggle which always ends in vexation and defeat. When pursued under the most favourable circumstances the profits of farming are but small and very precarious. The charm of agricultural life is certainly not the prospect of great pecuniary gain, but rather that sense of freedom and pleasure so intimately allied with the cultivation of the ground. The allurements to pastoral life are great, but if anything will enable a man of capital and common sense to resist them it is the knowledge that all his labour will be rendered useless by rabbits, which get rid of all uncertainty respecting profits by making them an impossibility. The best class of farmers will not work at a loss, and as quickly as possible they withdraw the remnant of their capital from the land, and send their sons into professions and businesses already over-crowded, but where, at any rate, there is something like a fair field. Grass land is burnt by rabbits to an extent scarcely credible by anyone who has not seen the bare brown places where they congregate. Corn crops are devoured and trodden down, but perhaps the greatest devastation is caused among turnips. Turnips eaten through the rind by rabbits rot on exposure to frost that has no effect whatever on the untouched roots. These are the immediate penalties paid by the farmer, but the landlord does not escape. Rabbits, wherever they are found, prevent pheasants from prospering; but this can be remedied to some extent by rearing rabbits on tenants' land, and pheasants in the landlords' covers. This is a convenient if not very equitable arrangement. In winter especially rabbits destroy young trees by barking them. The loss in this respect is great now, and would be much greater if planting were as common as it ought to be, and will be in a few years. Then there is the deterioration of the land and the still more important and irremediable deterioration of the tenants. These last-named are slow processes which do not quickly attract attention by making a great noise, nor yet by the suddenness of the changes they accomplish, but they are very real.

That the old class of tenant farmer is dying out is not disputed, and with him, unfortunately, is dying the old desire to cultivate the land as an honourable business. If Wales were canvassed it would probably be found that the low estimation in which agriculture is held is due mainly to ground game and absence of leases. It would also be discovered that in the Principality farming is despised as an occupation to an extent unknown in other parts of the United Kingdom. The holdings in Wales were always smaller than elsewhere. The creation of large farms that caused such an outcry in England has been to some extent necessitated in Wales by the slackness of demand for farms and by the inability or unwillingness of landowners to re-build homesteads.

It must not be understood that when a farm is to let in Wales there are no applicants for it. There are applicants, but they are not experienced farmers possessed of capital, nor the sons of farmers anxious to introduce new and improved methods of cultivation. The applicants, as a rule, are poor men anxious, if possible, to get a little out of the land without putting anything into it. They are not anxious for leases, and not even averse to rabbits! This deterioration in tenant farmers is mainly due to rabbits, tenure, and the general hopelessness of their business. Except under very special circumstances men possessed of skill and capital, if they cannot obtain leases and are not allowed to keep down rabbits, remove to districts where, on these subjects, a little more light has penetrated. They are too wise to wait for the approach of sure and certain ruin. Just below them there is a class of men unable to move—poverty, or language, or sentiment binds them to the place. These struggle on as well as they can and take care that none of their children follow their footsteps. Lower down than these again are the men who live from hand to mouth, a hopeless and thriftless life. They sink with their surroundings, and at last are worse off than ordinary labourers on well-regulated estates. There are, it is scarcely necessary to say, landlords in Wales fully alive to the ruin brought upon the owners and cultivators of land by rabbits, who have handed them over without reserve to tenants. The invariable result of this policy is a better supply of winged game, a more plentiful supply of hares, and quite as many rabbits as are necessary for sport. When ground game is handed over to the tenants they are at once converted into gamekeepers, and, as a rule, like to show their landlord a good day's sport when he comes over their farms with his gun. The gain in winged game would be far more than made up for any sacrifice in rabbits, especially if the saving in gamekeepers was reckoned. Now every farmer is interested is repressing game as much as he can; then he would be interested within reasonable limits in preserving it. If landlords gave tenants the ground-game, leases would be more freely granted, and land, instead of decreasing in value, would become worth more every year.

It is sometimes said that as soon as a Welsh farmer

obtains a twenty-one years' lease he sits down contentedly under the impression that he need make no further effort of any kind. That this is scarcely a true representation of a Welsh farmer may be fairly presumed from his reluctance to accept a long lease, which he very well knows means hard work, increased responsibility, and systematic investment of labour and capital.

Rabbits, as a rule, mean yearly tenures, poor tenants impoverished landlords, and decaying properties, and the landlord who sets up in the business of rabbit merchant from choice may live to see his descendants following the same occupation from necessity. Agriculture in the Principality suffers enough from other drawbacks without being cursed by a plague of rabbits.

CHAPTER XV.

PLANTING—WALES A LAND OF FORESTS.

IN many parts of Wales the scarcity of timber is one of the first things that impresses a stranger, but there is ample evidence in Acts of Parliament, Royal concessions, history, names of places, and in the subsoil of the country, that the Principality for many ages was thickly wooded. Indeed, the woods of the country during the long warfare between the Welsh and English were as useful to the natives as fortresses, and as formidable to invaders as armed foes. The bleak, bare mountains were clothed with timber which afforded safe shelter to the hardy followers of the Welsh Princes, and presented an impenetrable barrier to the invading forces of successive English Kings. The silent forest depths were dreaded as much as the sudden war cries of the irrepressible chiefs, nor, it appears, were the woods used by the people only for protection—"All the King's subjects and friends," we read in an old Act of Parliament, "may pass freely on horse back or on foot, and with cattel, wares, or otherwise, through all or any of the forests in Wales, without payment of any unlawful exactions, or suffering any other damage whatsoever. And no forester or other shall commit any such offence, on pain to be tried for the same as robbers, before the Justices of Peace of the shire adjoining." It is pretty certain that the King's "subjects and friends" were not as free from molestation as they desired, or this Act would never have been passed. The Act continues— "Cattel which stray into any forest there (in Wales), and are challenged within a year and a day by the right owner shall be re-delivered unto him upon demand; and if the forester or other officer or farmer, there refuse to re-deliver them, they shall forfeit to such owner double the value of such cattel."

This is very satisfactory as a piece of law, but if ancient escheators were anything like their descendants of to-day, the claimants would not often recover estrays, and would rarely venture to enforce the penalty.

When Edward I. was engaged in contesting the possession of the country with Llywelyn, we read in history that "from Rhuddlan Castle, in which the King resided during the month of July, 1282, he sent orders to the Sheriffs of the neighbouring counties to provide, each according to its extent and population, hatchet-men, to cut down the woods and open passages for his army. Out of the Forest of Dean and county of Hereford, two hundred cutters and colliers came, under Gilbert de Clare, Earl of Gloucester. He also stimulated the zeal of his barons by grants of forfeited estates out of the four cantreds. It was about this time that Archbishop Peckam came on the second occasion into Wales on his mission of peace and reconciliation. Llywelyn was then at his palace, Garth Celyn or Aber, on the Conway; and the Welsh army was stationed on the heights of Penmaen Mawr, considered the strongest fortification which the Welsh possessed in the mountains of Snowdon, and capable of containing twenty thousand men. While these excellently-intended negociations for peace were fruitlessly protracted the hatchet-men were not idle. The oaks of the forest, which had defied the winds and storms of a thousand years, fell prostrate; roads were opened through which reinforcements to the King's already immense army followed each other in rapid succession. The King on November 1st left Rhuddlan, and advanced to Conway. In order to coop the Welsh up in Snowdon, he stationed his cavalry in the plains at the base of the mountains, and his infantry on the sides of the hills under cover of the woods." The Welsh journeyings of Archbishop Peckham, who has already been mentioned, it is stated in history, were "along bad roads and through deep forests." It was from these forests, which are mentioned in the records of almost every engagement with the English forces, that the Welsh made their sudden onslaughts and into them they retired when outnumbered or defeated. The "Domesday Book" describes many forests on the Welsh marches as used only to supply provender to huge herds of swine. Woodward's history of Wales states, "that at the end of the year 1110 Madog ab Rhiryd, finding the manners and condition of the Irish disagreeable, returned to Wales and hid himself in the woods in his uncle Jorwerth's lordship." An old triad says there are three things without which a country is not a good one— wood, stones, and springs of water. In the poems of Davydd ab Gwilym who lived about the year 1340 there are numerous references to the wooded nature of the country. He says:—

> The fair country of my love,
> Looks dense as one continuous grove;
> Her lofty woods with warblers teem.

Again:

> Oh, lavish blossoms with thy hand
> O'er all the forests of the land.

A volume of interesting Welsh Sketches, published in 1852, contains many references to the forests of Wales. After describing the experiences of Edward I. and the successes of the Earl of Warwick, the writer refers to the reverses that befel Madoc of Shrewsbury about the year 1294, and says, "from that time the Welsh began to attend to the cultivation of the soil, the profits of commerce, and the arts of peace. "To this date is assigned the wholesale destruction of woods through Wales, wherein in any time of danger the natives in arms were wont to hide and save themselves." The laws of Howell Dda provide that "verdant woodland is to lie in tillage four years." Lady Guest's *Mabinogion* contains numerous references to the forests which in ancient times covered the country, and afforded hunting grounds in times of peace, and much-needed shelter during war. "Pwyll, Prince of Dyved," we are told in one of the stories, "was lord of the seven Cantrevs of Dyved, and once upon a time he was at Narberth, his chief palace, and he was minded to go and hunt, and the part of his dominions in which it pleased him to hunt was Glyn Cuch. So he set forth from Narbeth that night, and went as far as Llwyn Diarwyd. And that night he tarried there, and early on the morrow he rose and

came to Glyn Cuch ; when he let loose the dogs in the
wood and sounded the horn, and began the chase," &c.
Stags were the game, and enchanted castles and ladies
were more common than foxes in these degenerate days.
In the language, too, there is abundant proof in the
frequent appearance of the word "coed," where not a tree
survives, that at a former period the word described
woods which have since disappeared. In every district
there are dozens of places named in ways that indicate
the former existence of woods. Again, in some of the
old churches of the country there are records and traditions that permission was given in old times to cut
wood from the royal forests to repair sacred edifices. In
drainage works, railway cuttings, bogs, &c., trunks of
trees, hazel nuts, and masses of decayed vegetation are
found. On the surface in other places a few trees, the
stunted descendants of former forests, still survive.

When old houses and churches are taken down, they
are found to contain an amount of solid oak that certainly would never have been used if wood had not
been very much more plentiful then than now. It is
also clear from the permission given in some of the old
laws to cut trees near the sea "whose tops were
withered," that trees grew thickly down to the shore
in many parts of the Principality.

It is a curious fact that on the tops of comparatively
high hills the land is ridged as if corn had been grown
there in old times. According to legends still extant
in the country the valleys were full of trees, and it was
only possible to grow corn on the level places on the
hills which were perhaps also chosen because they were
freer than the valleys from the raids of enemies. There

is another fact that may be mentioned. Before the time of Elizabeth it was customary to give the poor in Wales leave to cut certain quantities of wood, a form of relief which would not have been adopted if wood had been anything like as scarce as it was only some forty years ago. During the last century in many parts of Wales the remaining portions of the old forests were cut down to provide fuel for smelting furnaces. It was easier to bring the ore to the timber than to take the timber to the ore. There are places called "The Forge" where very old people remember smelting furnaces to have existed.

CHAPTER XVI.

PLANTING—THE REVIVAL OF ARBORICULTURE.

AFTER the Principality had been almost completely stripped of its timber, hundreds of years elapsed and no attempt was made to replace the forests which had been cut down. It is not improbable that the clearing away of the ancient woods was deemed rather a good thing at the time than otherwise for the country, especially as fuel, other than wood or peat, was scarce and dear.

The development of mining, the construction of railways, the increasing scarcity of timber in all parts of the United Kingdom, and other causes, induced Welsh landlords to turn their attention to arboriculture for the first time about forty years ago. In Scotland tree planting was extensively pursued before the commencement of the present century, and it is not too much to say that a good deal of the agricultural prosperity of the country north of the Tweed may be attributed to the fact that when railways were first taken into Scotland there were extensive plantations ready for thinning. Landowners sold their timber at high prices, and were enabled to make improvements which in Wales are still withheld because of poverty. That planting in Wales was not so extensively adopted in the early part of the century is not surprising, but that it should be necessary in the last quarter of the century to adduce arguments in favour of tree planting is a strong proof of the backwardness of the country. When the agriculture of the Principality is unfavourably compared with that of Scotland and England, it is customary to plead that Wales is less favoured than other parts of the United Kingdom in soil and climate. As regards the growth of timber, however, there can be no doubt that Wales is without a rival, and the naked state of the country must therefore be attributed to some other cause than the poverty of the soil.

About the year 1809, a treatise was printed "On the Theory and Practice of Planting Forest Trees in every description of Soil and Situation, more particularly on Elevated Sites, Barren Heaths, Rocky Soils, &c." This treatise says, "it may be objected that the increase in the value of land furnishes an argument against planting; which is reasonably admitted, so far as lands of a middle value are concerned, and where shelter and ornament add nothing to value. But are there not numerous situations on almost every estate, which in themselves produce but little, and mock the darings of the cautious cultivator—which only require to be planted with judgment to become abundantly productive in timber? And are not the situations likewise numerous where planting becomes absolutely necessary on account of its shelter? Nor are instances wanted where a bare, flat surface of country may be so diversified and ornamented by patches of planting as to add to the real or saleable value of the property, abundantly more than the expense, besides the marketable value of the wood."

There are miles of land in Wales which produces nothing but scant herbage for a few sheep, but which is admirably adapted for larch, and if judiciously planted would produce a profitable crop of excellent timber for which there is an unfailing demand. A hundred years ago foreign timber fetched higher prices than that grown at home, but now English larch and Scotch fir command more money than Baltic timber of kindred sorts. Railways and improved roads have enabled the owners of plantations to dispose of their timber in distant markets, but the ever-increasing local demand for railway sleepers, telegraph poles, pitwood, hurdles, &c., has greatly reduced the necessity for seeking distant purchasers. The need for the shelter afforded by plantations is great in Wales. In winter fierce winds and heavy rains sweep the valleys, which lie exposed to every change of weather. Sheep and cattle have to face winter storms and summer heat, unrelieved by the shelter trees would afford.

The loss from want of protection against the weather is far more serious than farmers realize, and the shelter afforded by a belt of trees is incalculably greater than is generally supposed. A screen of timber grown at the entrance to a valley, or at the top of a hill, will do much to prevent that unbroken sweep of wind and rain which Welsh farmers have good cause to dread.

The treatise already quoted says—"On steeps, trees are more sheltered than on levels of equal elevation. In considering this matter, two points of the compass are out of the question, as when the wind blows along the steep, its effects must be much the same as from blowing along levels. When it blows from behind, or down such steep, there will be a calm among the trees except such as are near the summit. But to counterbalance this advantage it may be supposed that when the wind blows up the steep, its force will be considerably augmented by what is added in the ascent, which certainly must be the case, as long as the surface is somewhat bare. The matter, however, becomes materially different as soon as the trees get a few feet high; as from that time the wind has to travel over a sort of hollow surface, and in doing so, great part of it sinks in, and dies away among the branches." This may appear somewhat fanciful, but there is a good deal of force in what is said.

In some districts a little hedgerow timber is found, but so deep is the prejudice of farmers against trees that landlords are asked to remove them because they "poison" the land and harbour birds! The farmer says there is never any grass near the trees, but he forgets that the absence of grass may be accounted for by the tramping of the cattle which come there for shelter. The badly fenced condition of a large portion of Wales is partly due to the scarcity of timber. Poles are so dear that the tenant will not buy them and pay carriage. There are not trees enough on scores of holdings to supply the fields with posts and gates.

The absence of trees in Wales gives the country a sterile look which contrasts unfavourably with the park-like appearance of the Midland Counties of England. That nearly every kind of timber will grow in Wales scarcely needs to be proved; but if proof is necessary, it can be found in noble trees sparsely scattered all over the country. If waste corners, hedge rows, thin places, high grounds, and steep side-lands were planted, tenants would be greatly benefitted by the increased shelter, and landowners in less than twelve years would be able to insist upon fences and gates, without which profitable farming is impossible. In addition to spare pieces of land on ordinary farms, there are vast tracts which can only be made really profitable by planting, and the question why these tracts are not planted naturally arises.

Here and there a landlord is doing all he can to plant waste lands, but there are others who never plant a tree. Wherever an estate on the death of the present holder passes to a distant male branch of the family there is little prospect of the tenant for life spending money in planting or in improvements of any kind. The Earl of Lisburne is a great planter, and in this respect is following the example of the previous Earl, who planted the Crosswood hills, which are now clothed with fine larch and Scotch fir. Sir Pryse Pryse, the owner of Gogerddan, is planting more freely than formerly, but Sir Watkin, the largest landowner in Wales, now plants little or nothing. Sir Edmund Buckley has planted large tracts in Montgomeryshire and Merionethshire. In the north and south considerable attention is now paid to arboriculture, but there is more to be done than this generation can possibly accomplish. There is not a mountain in Wales which would not grow larch if the capital were forthcoming. Unfortunately most of the landowners are poor, and cannot afford to wait thirty or forty years for a crop, however profitable.

It often happens that for want of labour plantations are left unthinned and unfenced until great injury has been done. There is ample room in Wales for safe and profitable investment of capital in planting timber and properly attending to the crop until ready for the market. Welsh patriotism, it is to be regretted, seldom takes the form of desiring to obtain possession of land, and still more seldom of improving and beautifying it. Considering the short time planting has been in favour in Wales, much has been done to lay down plantations, but there is nothing in the country approaching to forests. The woods are still young, the bulk of them under twenty years' growth. Every year thousands of acres are planted, and several of the large landowners rear plants in nurseries on their estates. Notwithstanding this home growth, however, professional nurserymen find the demand for larch and other conifers is almost greater than can be met. In no department of agriculture, perhaps, is the present condition of the country more hopeful than in tree planting. Those landlords who are too poor to embark in laying down wood are loud in praise of planting, and urge poverty as the only admissible excuse for not planting the hills, which now add nothing to the rental, but which would pay better than the best land on the estate if covered with larch, and protected by borders of Scotch fir. The only hope for some of the poor, embarrassed landowners of Wales lies in planting their land. But many of them are so fond of rabbits, and so anxious to maintain a reputation as lovers of sport, that they prefer poverty with a gun on its shoulder to competence with no rabbits on the land. Rabbits, to the long list of their evil doings, must be set down as the most destructive and determined enemies of young trees, and when allowed to run among them, add materially to the cost of planting.

CHAPTER XVII.

PLANTING—THE FUTURE OF ARBORICULTURE.

ABOUT the year 1800 foreign timber in this country began to be much dearer than at any previous time, and English trees, resorted to on account of their cheapness, contrary to expectation, were found to be equal to the foreign sorts. Scotch fir then fetched about half, and poles about a third as much as foreign timber. Spruce fir, which had been planted up to this period chiefly for shelter and ornament, began to claim attention on the ground of profit, but as the seedlings were dear, this tree was at first too expensive for general planting, and had also to contend with strong adverse prejudice. Increased demand for a forest tree, as is well known, tends to diminish its cost, and consequently as spruce fir grew in popularity, it came more within the reach of planters. Scotch fir, again, called the planter's forlorn hope, and formerly valued chiefly as a nurse for other trees, grows well on sites exposed to particular currents of wind, and is often the only tree that will grow at all. It does not shrink even from the sea breeze, but grows in full luxuriance near the shore. How true this is may be seen by anyone in different parts of the Principality where this tree has been liberally planted during recent years.

It has been urged against planting that woods may be so extended as to encroach upon land required for agriculture. There is little danger of this result anywhere, and less, perhaps, in the Principality, where so many thousands of acres are fit for nothing but wood, than in any other portion of the United Kingdom. It is clear that as long as British timber is worth more per foot than foreign, there is no risk in growing wood, and if some of the poorer grazing lands were planted, and arable land was converted into pasture, there are unlimited corn depots in various parts of the world where grain can be purchased more cheaply, and of better quality than can be grown in the Principality. There is, however, little danger in Wales that plantations will encroach on ordinary agricultural land, and it should not be forgotten that woods by affording shelter improve the value of the agricultural land in their vicinity; indeed some large landowners have said that by planting broad screens, fields have been made worth three times as much as they were before. This is, perhaps, the exaggeration of enthusiasts, but it will be admitted that trees are valuable for the shelter they afford, and that an estate is enhanced in value if well wooded, apart from the market price of the trees. There is a tendency, perhaps, in these days, to plant only one or two sorts of quick-growing timber, but it should not be forgotten that mixed plantations are profitable for the reason that some trees seek their nutriment in the sub-soil, whilst others come near the surface for sustenance. Besides, when a plantation is mixed, the slower growths may be left to reach maturity, and to adorn the estate on which they grow.

It may reasonably be asked whether there is not some danger of overstocking the market with timber if planting continues to grow in favour with landowners for another quarter of a century, as it has grown in the past. Nothing is surer than that the reckless destruction of timber in America and elsewhere will sooner or later make itself felt in higher prices for English wood. Forests once destroyed, cannot be replaced by mere expenditure of money and labour. Time, that must be patiently waited for, is the chief thing in the growth of woods, which, like many other precious things, are often not rightly valued until they have been destroyed. It took centuries to rear them, and it will require centuries to replace them.

Mr. Samuel Roberts, Llanbrynmair, a veteran Welsh writer, who at some time or other has broken a lance at every kind of wrong, in an article on "Old Trees" once said, "the proprietors of the hills and dales of our country have done vast injury to their estates, and thereby occasioned heavy losses to their families, and inflicted grievous wrongs on their tenants, by neglecting the laws of Timber Cultivation. They have wofully neglected this important department of their duty and interest in various ways." The writer then goes on to calculate the loss which has accrued from allowing trees to "cumber the ground" after they had reached maturity. With this part of the article few lovers of old trees will altogether agree, even if they are able to believe in all the loss of accumulated interest, amounting to millions of pounds, caused by not cutting down a tree worth ten shillings as soon as it was ripe!

From whatever point the subject is looked at, it is clear the interest of landowners lies in planting the rougher portions of their estates with forest trees. The investment is a good one, and one that a man may make according to his means. If he cannot plant fifty acres a year let him plant one, and he will find that he has not only put his money where it will return good interest, but has occupied himself in a labour that gives him a claim to public regard. An enthusiastic writer on arboriculture says—"A thriving plantation, however misplaced, becomes, with the bulk of mankind, an object of regard, approaching almost to veneration." He further shrewdly remarks that "perhaps the idea of utility inseparably connected with such objects goes far in stamping the impression." For shelter trees are absolutely necessary, not only for cattle, but for the land itself, and ought to be utilized for this purpose far more extensively than they are. For ornamentation clumps and belts of trees are invaluable. They add to the apparent size of a park, and increase the attractiveness of a landscape. As a crop they are more profitable than almost anything else, and are essentially a landlord's crop.

It is not within the scope of the writer to enter into details on profits, but it may be observed that trees are admitted to be a crop that pays a good rent, returns fair interest on the capital invested, and in addition leaves a balance of profit besides the increased value of the land on which the trees were grown. In conclusion, there is one point which may be referred to. The demand for trees in towns is growing, and already in some parts of Wales streets are enlivened by bright foliage. This is a department in which only a beginning has yet been made by public bodies, but in watering places more particularly every available piece of ground ought to be planted with suitable trees—not a tree here and there, but liberally. Private persons, too, who have a piece of ground behind their houses might plant a tree or two, and Town Councils and Local Boards ought certainly to do something to redeem their reputation for encouraging ugliness, by promoting the planting of trees in streets, squares, and open spaces. The man has yet to be found who does not admit that trees are pleasant to look at, especially in towns where they pleasantly break "the long, unlovely street.'

CHAPTER XVIII.

LABOUR SAVING MACHINERY.

THAT labour saving machinery is not more common in Wales is due partly to the fact that hitherto agricultural implement makers and agents have not canvassed the country as completely as other parts of the Kingdom are canvassed. Nor are makers and agents altogether to blame for this. Even now a large portion of the Principality must be travelled over without the assistance of railways, and a still greater obstacle is found in the fact that before the implement maker's representative can hope to make headway, he must be able to speak the language of the people. In addition to the absence of railways and the presence of the Welsh language, the implement manufacturer has to deal with a poor and scattered population who earn a scant living by working an exhausted soil in primitive ways.

Although wooden ploughs are becoming scarcer every year, they may still be found in out-of-the-way places amongst the hills of the Principality, where farming is carried on with startling disregard of scientific, economic, and other principles generally supposed to be universally acknowledged and obeyed. The thrashing machine has superseded the flail more completely than mowers and reapers have superseded sickles and scythes, but the flail is not yet obsolete, although the hiss and whirr and rattle of the engine and thresher are no longer strange sounds among the Welsh hills. In a variable climate, where rain is frequent, the most approved hay makers and horse rakes, it might be thought, would be in great request. Nothing of the kind. Two men with their scythes will turn into a six-acre field and work away among the grass and stones with praiseworthy assiduity and patience. The value of one man's labour may be altogether wasted owing to the neglect in not picking the stones in the spring. If remonstrated with, the farmer would probably excuse himself by explaining that in the spring there is always so much to do, and extra help is so difficult to get, that this particular field was left unpicked. The reason why he does not get a patent mower is that the stones are unpicked, and he does not see the use of obtaining a haymaker as long as he is compelled to have men on the ground to cut the grass. Not unfrequently when the stones are gathered into heaps they are left on the field for years, sad evidences of carelessness.

The first cost of labour-saving machinery is the great obstacle that stands between the farmer and the manufacturer. It is easier for the farmer to pay a man half-a-crown or three shillings a day for a month or six weeks every year, than to pay £10 or £15 down for a machine that will do the work in two days, under the guidance of a man at the same wages. The expenditure of £100 in the erection of a turbine might not only save endless labour, but make that possible which is now impossible; but in the first place the tenant is not in possession of the £100, and in the second he is only a yearly tenant, and would not venture upon an expenditure which might result in a rise of rent, and perhaps a notice to quit. The farmer, therefore, goes on cutting food by hand just as his fathers did before him, with the result that he cannot make profit out of keeping stock, the preparation of whose food is a far more serious item than it was fifty years ago, when his competitors were unable to obtain the mechanical aids he now neglects to use. No farmer who means to make profit should take a holding unless he can arrange with his landlord for the erection of a turbine, waterwheel, or windmill to drive his machinery, unless he is in a position to purchase a steam engine. An antiquated hay chopper, minus a blade, is better than nothing, but only just. A man and a boy by working hard can prepare food in a day which, with a modern machine and the use of steam, wind, or water, would be prepared by the boy himself in half an hour. Pulpers, slicers, crushers, chaff cutters, &c., not only reduce the cost of a given amount of labour, but make it possible to get through a very much larger amount.

A considerable number of farming operations must, it is well known, be performed within a given time if the work is to be profitable. A writer on the advantages of steam cultivation, when dealing with this fact, says—" Steam does the work at the proper time. However great the area to be cultivated, the speed and power of steam cultivation will overtake it. Whether ten or a thousand acres are required to be turned up in autumn for wheat or winter frost, it can all be overtaken by steam in time to ensure the benefit sought. The same thing cannot be done by horses, unless at such an expenditure of horse flesh, horse food, horsemen, and horse implements as renders it practically impossible by the ordinary strength of the farm."

What will Welsh farmers, who believe in three-inch ploughing, say to the following extract from the same author—"Steam does the work effectually, and to the required depth, which animal power cannot always do. It is plain that animal power is limited, and that the depth stirred thereby must necessarily be limited to the power of the animals employed. It is equally plain that steam power applied to cultivation is practically unlimited, and that the power of steam can be commanded to stir to any depth above the bare rocks. It will generally be admitted that it would be very beneficial to the farmer to have his clay soils occasionally stirred to a depth of eighteen or twenty inches—better to thirty—but this is practically impossible by animal power, though quite possible by steam power. In some parts of England clay soils are cultivated three feet deep, by thirty-horse power engines, and grow in consequence great crops. Steam power has cultivated effectually to any required depth, and to such depths as are quite impracticable by animal power."

The first cost is considerable, but the advantages of steam cultivation are great. The breadth ploughed per bout by one set of Fowler's twelve-horse power steam tackle is generally equal to the overturn of twelve horses. The Right. Hon. the Earl of Dunmore, F.R.G.S., in a published letter on Steam Cultivation, says, "It would take up too much space were I to attempt to describe to you all the different systems now in operation; they are all good, and they are all the results of experiments conducted by men who have given their whole time and thought to the subject, and to whom too much praise cannot be given. Amongst the most noted of these agricultural engineers, are the Howards of Bedford; Amies, Barford, & Co. of Peterboro'; and Barrows & Stewart of Banbury, who work Mr. William Smith's (of Woolston) patent; this latter gentleman was one of the earliest pioneers of steam-culture, and to his untiring energy the agriculturists of England owe a debt of gratitude. No sooner does a farmer see with his own eyes the excellence of the work, the speed with which it is effected, than he immediately wants the steam plough on his own farm. The question is, How is he to get it? Very few farmers have the capital to invest in a set of tackle; therefore the only way that steam cultivation can be placed within their reach is, by private companies being got up by lardlords and influential farmers in the different districts of the United Kingdom, and letting out steam-cultivating implements for hire to all farmers, large or small."

Steam ploughs, water wheels, steam engines, turbines, mowers and reapers, improved horse ploughs, grubbers, drills, slicers, pulpers, and crushers, which cost nothing to keep and are always ready for use, enable the farmer to do his work in the best style and just when it ought to be done. The saving in preparing food for horses, cattle, and sheep by machinery, instead of by hand, is very great; but that is nothing to the saving effected by getting ground prepared for seed at the right time, and in securing the crops as soon as they are ready for harvesting. Every hay harvest a good deal of grass is left uncut until half its nutriment is lost by over-ripeness, simply because the farmer is unable with his primitive appliances to secure his crops at the right time. To complete the loss, the crop, when at last mown, is left on the ground until it is withered and worth little except for bedding.

One of the reasons why turnips and mangels are not more extensively grown in Wales is, that the ground requires more preparation than the average farmer, with his antiquated methods, can give it, without neglecting the ordinary work on the land. In autumn, wheat, oats, and barley are often left in the fields until the grain drops out of the husks, and, after the crop is cut, the remaining portion of the grain is soaked again and again before it is finally garnered. With the present restricted supply of labour, it behoves farmers to provide themselves with machinery, so that they can get through a press of work either at seed time or harvest, by merely putting on an extra machine, which will do the work of eight or ten men. In this as in other matters, there is a spirit of improvement abroad. Machines and implements sell far more freely now than they sold ten years ago, notwithstanding the fact that manufacturers do not make special efforts to increase the sale. At agricultural shows in Wales it seldom happens there is more than one stand of implements and machinery exhibited, and not infrequently there is no exhibition of this kind at all. This fact is to be regretted for the farmer's sake, and it is not one that can be considered beneficial to implement makers and agents.

Agricultural shows are now common all over Wales,

and implement manufacturers might make an allowance to their agents towards the expense of conveying implements to shows, and keeping them at work during the time the public are admitted to the show yards. In England, and in some parts of Wales, agents find it pays them to do this on their own account, but as a rule in many parts of Wales the carriage of the machines is an item of expense that would exceed perhaps the profit on a year's sales. It is unfortunate that Welsh farmers who do not think of going to the Royal Show, and who have little faith in new-fangled machines, seldom have the opportunity at their local shows of seeing at work machines and implements which would in many instances pay for themselves in one year. The practice of some large landowners of sending their tenants to the Royal Agricultural Show is one that might be extensively followed with great advantage. One drawback, in a poor country, against the introduction of improved machinery is found in its dearness, but this might be got over as regards steam ploughs by combination.

CHAPTER XIX.

AGRICULTURAL SOCIETIES.

THE tendency everywhere among the uneducated is to care more for money than for money's worth, and in Wales, owing formerly to the greater scarcity of specie than of other forms of wealth, this tendency was developed and confirmed to an extent worthy of note, especially among rural populations, where very curious instances of its survival to the present time can still be found. A farmer otherwise intelligent will allow five pounds worth of manure to run into his drains, but will not pay five shillings either to save it or to buy fresh; he will in a week give ten shillings worth of food and attention to a horse which he need not keep at all if he could only bring himself to pay an occasional half-crown for the hire of a horse just when he wanted it; he will keep an old cow from sentiment, and will at last waste half-a-day at the fair in haggling over two shillings, in its price, but he will not spend five shillings in securing a well bred sire, nor any sum in fitting an animal for the market. He will give a day's work to anybody, but the price of one to nobody. He is, in short, hampered on all hands by an exaggerated sense of the value of money. He prefers a sovereign in coin rather than a medal twice or three times its value, and he saves money by purchasing second rate seeds and breeding third rate cattle. Even if he wants a lease the value of which he well understands he can seldom bring himself to volunteer an advance of rent equal to say ten or fifteen per cent, but he will lose without a murmur three or four times fifteen per cent. by working from hand to mouth on a farm held on yearly tenure. He likes that dearest of all articles—a low-priced auctioneer, too, and never seems to think there is anything about an auctioneer, except his licence, different from other men. He loses considerably in this way, and also by his desire for cheap lawyers and doctors. He would readily give a lawyer a sheep for a deed, but, in money, will only give five shillings to a clerk or a schoolmaster, and so frequently gets not only a deed, but a lawsuit! The rule on Welsh farms is to take the greatest possible care of money and to waste produce, and that which would result in produce, as if it had no money value whatever.

A farmer who would not on any account give a blacksmith a penny more than the regulation sum for shoeing a horse will spend the best part of a day himself in going with it to the blacksmith's shop, and waiting until the horse is ready to take back again. He has in fact not realized the adage that time is money, and produce is wealth. Hard cash he can understand, but time and the results of labour he treats as of little value. He is liberal with them, and if he gets out of poverty it is only by dint of hard saving, and at the expense of much suffering.

This misapprehension as to the value of money forms one of the chief difficulties the promoters of agricultural societies have to contend with in their efforts to improve the cultivation of the country. Prize lists have to be arranged, not so much with regard to the improvement of stock and crops as to the best means of giving prizes to the largest number of exhibitors. Farmers have not yet learnt that agricultual shows benefit them, whether they win prizes or not, and cannot understand that those exhibitors reap most advantage from an agricultural society who have no chance whatever of obtaining prizes. It is perfectly ridiculous in the eyes of ordinary farmers to subscribe towards the funds of an agricultural society from which they have no hope of obtaining prizes. How they can be benefitted by shows at which they are not even exhibitors is beyond their comprehension. Of course the mere gathering together of the stock and produce of a district is a means of education farmers cannot afford to despise, especially in these days when it is only by adopting the best methods that farmers can hope to hold their own in that competition which is not now confined to English or even European markets. This is what needs to be enforced time after time and in all sorts of ways. There is scarcely a trace of that healthy rivalry among the exhibitors which, if it could once be originated, would do far more than prizes to stimulate agriculturists to take pride in their business. The "highly commended" award of judges is not nearly so highly valued as a fourth or fifth prize would be in money. Much needs to be done towards convincing average farmers that agricultural societies are established and carried on chiefly to benefit tenants by showing them what their neighbours are doing to make the soil more fruitful and stock-breeding more profitable.

A good deal of an agricultural society's usefulness is lost because the chief promoters will not take care that the speeches at the annual dinner are of a practical kind. On the day of the show it is perhaps not possible for the exhibitors to sit and listen comfortably to speeches. They have their exhibits to attend to, and are often very tired. A day might, however, easily be fixed for the distribution of prizes, a cheap dinner might be provided, and good speeches might be delivered which would exercise beneficial influence upon the minds of the members. The advantages of agricultural societies to those who do not win prizes, the need for recognizing the money-value of time, farm-yard manure, neglected pieces of land, briar-pulled wool, the folly of buying second-rate seeds, the loss entailed by growing weeds, especially with root crops, the advantage of breeding pure-bred stock, the profit to be made out of judicious feeding. These, and scores of other subjects, might be touched upon with great appropriateness at the annual dinners of Welsh agricultural societies. Instead of that, a number of well-worn platitudes are uttered, and nobody is a single thought the better. The loss caused by the purchase of cheap seeds is especially a point that agricultural societies might well pay attention to. Encouragement should be given in every possible way to those who sell new seeds, and farmers ought to be instructed how to judge. There is an idea that, although fresh well cleaned seeds are better than old and dirty sorts, the difference is not sufficient to turn the balance in favour of the more expensive kinds.

There is another thing which might be done to make the beneficial effects of agricultural societies more generally felt. The judges of farms and green crops usually send in written awards containing useful criticisms and observations on what they saw in their tour of inspection. If judges of horses, cattle, sheep, and pigs were also expected to send in to the secretaries written reports containing criticisms and general observations, the result would be a useful mass of information which, if circulated, would guide farmers, and would tend to the discovery of faults and remedies. Some of the judges would not report in detail, but from time to time useful hints would be obtained, and one object of every good agricultural society should be to get rid of prejudices and superstitions concerning the land and its treatment, by circulating sound information respecting the best methods. A society has certainly not done all its duty when it has arranged a show, and distributed a good round sum in prizes. Exhibitors who have no merit, are not passed over by the judges as often as they ought to be, and "highly commended" awards are scattered about far too liberally.

The Welsh farmer can only succeed as he is able to compete with, and excel, farmers in other parts of the country. Of course he will not try to fatten Shropshire sheep on high side-land farms, nor will he obtain the heaviest of Norfolk horses for hilly districts, but he will do his utmost to discover what is best adapted for the country, and will bring that as speedily as possible to perfection. In these efforts he will be assisted by the district agricultural society, which ought to give prizes for those breeds of animals, and those kinds of produce which deserve to be encouraged, and not for anything that happens to have come down from times when a system prevailed adapted for a condition of things now passed away. In Wales, for instance, it is very doubtful whether any society ought to encourage the growth of wheat by giving prizes for it. Occasionally a good crop of wheat may be raised, but oats or barley would be more profitable, and additional roots are urgently needed.

CHAPTER XX.

LIME AND BONES.

TENANT farmers, liable on short notices to be turned out of their holdings, or, what they dread perhaps still more, to have their rents raised, are not likely to expend much capital in bones and lime. This fact is so obvious that Welsh landowners cannot be ignorant of it and yet they persistently decline to make twenty-one year leases the rule instead of the exception. A yearly tenant who limed and bone-manured his land liberally; who drained wet places, and kept watercourses, ditches, and drains well open; who cut and repaired fences and kept up gates; who made roads through his farm, and maintained his house and buildings in good repair; who procured good implements, and saved manual labour by erecting a water-wheel, windmill, turbine, or steam engine; who grew turnips and mangels; who fattened stock, and sent his children to first-class schools: a yearly tenant who acted in this way would be looked upon as a lunatic by the public, and would very soon be told by his landlord that his rent was too low by half.

When £10 or £15 an acre had been spent on the land the tenant would be removed, or his rent would be raised equal perhaps to ten per cent. on the amount he had expended of his own capital. There are landlords—but they are scarce—who would neither evict an improving tenant nor raise his rent, but a good business man engaged in agriculture cannot invest his capital without security, and there is no security like that afforded by a long lease and freedom to keep down ground game, and to crop the ground as he finds it to be to his advantage. Farming, without lime and bones, is very much like the children of Israel's brickmaking without straw—thankless labour. The only thing required to complete the tenant's hopeless condition is that his homestead should be erected, as thousands of homesteads in Wales are erected, on the side of a hill, and that the fertilizing qualities should be washed out of the farmyard manure into blocked drains! The results will be disease in his household, much labour in carting the ruined manure upon his fields, and scant crops. The loss of manure entailed by the position of the farmyard of course cannot be attributed to the farmer; nor, in the present state of education in Wales, can he be severely blamed for his indifference to that loss, and his neglect to minimize it.

The average Welsh farmer, as is pointed out in a preceding chapter, at once understands the loss of a dead sheep or of a sovereign in money, but he fails altogether to realize the far greater loss of rain-drenched manure, bad seed, or underfed cattle. It cannot be expected that a tenant who does not zealously guard his farmyard manure from deterioration will be the first to recognize the need for careful treatment of lime and the desirability of liberal expenditure in bones. Indeed the agriculturist whose education has been neglected can only with great difficulty be made to understand that the material for the supply of crops must be regularly put into the soil or the time will come when that material will be exhausted and the land will become valueless. Lime is scarce and dear in many parts of Wales, but the wasteful treatment to which it is subjected might induce a stranger to think it was obtained free of cost. The process of slaking is often left to the rain, and the lime is then not used until it has lost most of its caustic qualities. A paragraph on this subject from Professor Tanner's useful little work needs to be enforced on Welsh farmers with all the emphasis that can be commanded. "There are two methods," says the author referred to, "by which caustic lime is slaked. One of these is a bad and wasteful system, and the other is a good and economical plan. It is a too common practice for lime which has been drawn for manure to be distributed over the land in small heaps, and left there until the rain has slaked it. This not only leads to much delay, but as the slaking takes place gradually, much of the lime has been acted upon by the carbonic acid of the atmosphere, and much of its power lost before it is brought into use. Compare with this the care taken by a mason when slaking lime for mortar: no delay is allowed; it is done quickly by adding sufficient water, and then it is heaped up and covered from the air by sand. Some farmers adopt the same plan, and as soon as the heaps are made in the field a water cart carries round the water required for the proper slaking of the lime, and it is then heaped up and protected from the air by a covering of earth. For building purposes it is necessary to slake the lime thoroughly and without loss, and it is equally so for use as a manure. The only difference is that the loss is more easily detected in the case of the builder, but it is equally a loss to the farmer, whether he knows it or not. Lime is, after all, an expensive manure before it is got upon the land, and it is unwise to allow it to waste."

On the side-land farms of Wales lime is far more expensive manure than on the level tracts of England, but the tenants of those side-land farms who carefully study how to make the most of the lime they purchase are certainly a small minority. Instead of covering up the slaked lime, and afterwards harrowing it into the land before its power has been abstracted by the atmosphere, the custom is to leave it on the fields until the weather has made it almost useless. That poor farmers should purchase lime, drag it laboriously up steep fields, and then fail to make the best possible use of it, is one of those extraordinary facts which can only be explained by the cultivator's ignorance of the properties and uses of the article he is dealing with. Lime, for obvious reasons, is far more generally used in Wales than bones. The yearly tenant knows that lime will assist him in getting out of the land, for a time at any rate, more than he puts into it. He will make the soil hungrier in the long run, but if landlords prefer yearly tenants and a certain territorial power, rather than leases and improved estates, the tenant must accommodate himself to the conditions of his position, and must study how to get crops without permanently improving his holding.

Half-inch bones are a costly manure that lasts, and consequently one that yearly tenants seldom use anywhere, and still more seldom in Wales. In some parts of the Principality not only are bones not put on the land, but they are carefully collected and sent away into England to be manufactured into manures, which do not find their way back again. The custom in Wales of sending away store stock which has hardly done growing is one that makes the greatest drain upon the land with the least return in the shape of manure. The bones sent away every year in the skins of animals are an item too often lost sight of by farmers who are slow to believe that Wales is as capable of improvement as the once bleak region north of the Tweed. There are towns in this part of the United Kingdom from which many tons of old bones are sent away every year instead of being ground and applied to the land.

A practical farmer of great experience is not required to understand that Wales is not in a position to send away bones in large quantities without feeling their loss. It may, however, be said that more than an equivalent for the bones sent away is returned in lime, superphosphates, and other manures. Except in rare instances, it is to be feared that this is not the case, especially among tenants. There are, of course, intelligent landowners, leaseholders, and freeholders, who deal generously with the soil, and who have found that it requites generosity with profitable crops, but the bulk of cultivators are yearly tenants, who risk nothing and reap nothing. They would not be justified in risking anything under a system of tenure that not only leaves them at the mercy of the landlord, but makes them the victims of accidents which happen with sufficient regularity to prevent any reasonable man from calculating on their non-occurrence.

The waste of farmyard manure, the mismanagement of quick lime, and the exportation of bones in one form or another are points well deserving the attention of farmers and landowners in every part of the Principality. If the soil of Wales is less kindly than that of England and Scotland, Welsh farmers should be more and not less careful to utilize every artificial aid for its improvement. If the English farmer finds it necessary on rich soil to husband his farmyard manure, to carefully slake and apply lime, to import bones, and to assiduously till the ground, then the Welsh farmer surely cannot afford to dispense with these things on poor land which has been neglected for generations. It is true that Wales is not like Kent or Norfolk, but Wales can be indefinitely improved by the mere application to agriculture of those ordinary business principles, without which nothing can be done in trade or commerce. If the soil of Wales is not naturally rich, the way to improve it is not to waste manure and let things drift, but to grapple with the conditions of the case, and study what is most likely to succeed. There are disabilities, but there are also advantages, and it is absurd to think that with security for the investment of capital, and freedom from ground-game, the tenant farmers of Wales could not put upon the country a different face than that it now wears. The great drawback to agriculture, due to the impression in the minds of tenants that good farming does not pay, makes itself in almost every department. There is in every district at least one enterprising man who takes the lead in cultivation, but his neighbours, instead of following his example, look upon him as a dangerous person whose evil courses are only to be studied to be shunned.

"The value of bones as a manure," writes Mr. Edward Purser, "is so well known that little need be said about them further than that the home supply is far too small for our requirements, and consequently we have had to look to foreign sources for a very large portion of the bones used; the importations, which in 1844 were about 40,000 tons per annum, now considerably exceed 100,000 tons. Raw bones being slow in their action, it was found desirable to use them in a partially dissolved state. For the method of doing so we are indebted to the researches of the late Professor Liebig, in whose 'Organic Chemistry' (translated by Dr. Lyon Playfair in 1840), the following passage occurs: 'The form in which they (bones) are restored to the soil does not appear to be a matter of indifference, for the more finely the bones are reduced to powder, and the more intimately they are mixed with the soil, the more easily are they assimilated. The most easy and practical mode of effecting their division is to pour over the bones in a state of pure powder their weight of sulphuric acid diluted with three or four parts of water, and after they had been digested for some time to add 100 parts of water, and sprinkle this mixture over the fields before the plough. Experiments instituted on a soil formed from Grauwacke for the purpose of ascertaining the action of manure thus prepared, have distinctly shown that neither corn nor kitchen garden plants suffer in consequence, but on the contrary, they thrive with much more vigour.'"

CHAPTER XXI.

HORSES.

TAKING the Principality altogether it may fairly be said that horses are considerably in advance of other live stock. They more nearly approach that standard of excellence which ought to be aimed at in every department of agriculture, and present an average of which there is no occasion to be ashamed. Wales is favourably known to horse dealers all over the United Kingdom, and at some of the large fairs well-bred animals of great power and fine action are exhibited and are quickly bought up at high prices for the English markets. Long before the formation of Agricultural Societies efforts were made in Wales to improve the breed of horses. Sometimes landlords and others acted together and imported sires, as in Montgomeryshire a hundred years ago, and in Cardiganshire until last year. Probably, however, that love of horseflesh and pride in a good animal which are as deeply ingrained in Welshmen as Yorkshiremen have had great influence in maintaining and improving the breed of horses.

In 1872 an association was formed at Aberystwyth for the purpose of improving the breed of horses in that county. At the dinner held after the first show, it was stated that prior to the Crimean War Cardiganshire was celebrated for horses, but that the breed had deteriorated between 1853 and and 1872 owing to the fact that farmers had sold their best animals during the war time, and that landowners at that period ceased to keep entire horses. The Cardiganshire Association was very successful for several years, and unquestionably did something towards bringing back the fame the county once possessed. Unfortunately the necessary funds could not be obtained for high premiums, and about two years ago the association ceased to exist. The Cardiganshire Agricultural Society, into which the Horse Association was merged, then offered a premium of £40 or £50 for the best stallion for agricultural purposes. The money offered, however, was not sufficient to attract good animals from beyond the Welsh border without a guarantee of mares, and therefore for two years a horse was practically engaged to travel the district for the premium and a guaranteed number of mares. The dissatisfaction of the farmers with the "foreign" horse was so great that last season (1878) a show of stallions was held, and the premium was awarded to one of the local horses.

The object of the Cardiganshire Horse Association was not to support local animals, but to improve them by importing fresh blood from other parts of the country. It is worthy of note that one of the arguments urged for awarding the premium to local horses was that the imported sires had improved the breed, and that the need for going out of Wales no longer existed. In short the success of the Horse Association was pleaded as a reason for its discontinuance. Several of the speakers at the dinner after the Agricultural Show in 1878, referred to the abandonment of the importation of sires, and spoke so strongly in favour of what the Horse Association had accomplished, that there is every reason to believe that in future at least one first class foreign horse will be engaged to travel Cardiganshire. The name of Mr. Vaughan Davies, Tanybwlch, near Aberystwyth, deserves to be remembered in connection with the effort to improve the breed of Cardiganshire horses.

In some districts of Wales landlords keep entire horses and contract for the privilege of buying the yearling colts at a certain sum fixed upon. This custom works well, exerts a beneficial influence on the breed of horses in the neighbourhoods where it is practised, and might with advantage be extended.

The Agricultural Societies all over the country offer prizes for entire horses, and in many districts there are also special shows for stallions. Unfortunately the money offered in prizes is not sufficient to attract animals from one county to another, much less from England or Scotland, nor is it sufficient to induce a farmer who happens to possess a rare animal not to sell him. As soon as a good horse is discovered in any part of the country a long price is sure to be offered for him, and the chances are that he changes hands. Under these circumstances it is clearly necessary to go to England, not only for fresh blood, but also for the best class of Welsh horses. If the best animals reared in Wales were kept there and were available for breeding purposes the need for importing sires would not be so pressing as it is, and those who contend strongly for local horses would have a much better chance of being listened to than there is any hope of under the present circumstances. The large landowners, it is true, retain good horses in their own hands, but many of them take pride in selling animals for large sums just to show what Wales can do in horseflesh.

Horse breeding is generally recognized to be a very important part of a farmer's business from a national point of view. From time to time in the House of Commons it is asserted with great confidence that the breed of horses is going to the dogs, and that unless something is done very speedily there will not be a horse worthy of the name in the country. This, like other national scares, comes round at irregular but frequent intervals, and passes away when some new topic comes to the front. The last occasion was when the Government purchased some horses in America for the Army Corps. All kinds of exaggerated rumours were then set afloat, and great consternation was expressed at the idea that this country should be compelled to go to America for horses. In some of these Parliamentary discussions Wales has been favourably mentioned as a portion of the United Kingdom where something of set purpose is done to improve the breed of horses. That Wales is well adopted for rearing strong hardy animals, well adapted for general purposes cannot be doubted, and every year farmers are becoming more and more alive to the profit that may be made out of really good brood mares, which happily are not scarce in Wales, though they are not always as well treated as they deserve to be.

The short legged, short bodied, compact cob, used for

hilly ground, and more particularly identified with Cardiganshire, commands a ready market. It is not particular about food, trots well, and takes a good load. The Montgomeryshire horse, much heavier and slower, is sought for hard work on level lands and in towns. The Carnarvon breed has recently grown in favour, and is well known and highly valued. Carmarthenshire shows up well in hunters, and other counties have their specialities. Merionethshire, for instance, was long celebrated for thoroughbreds, nor is the strain altogether lost even yet, although it is not found unmixed. Cardiganshire mountain ponies, too, are celebrated all over England. One of the chief fairs for them is Pontrhydfendigaid. So much has been done in the past, in first one part of the country and then another, that no doubt can exist that Wales is peculiarly adapted for rearing a hardy, useful breed of horses able to command good prices in the English market.

The horses on average are somewhat smaller perhaps than is desirable for farm work, but as the notion dies out that the land is too poor to support large horses— and especially as the land and roads are improved— heavier sorts will become commoner. Welsh horses purchased for the English markets are not as a rule used for draught, but for speed. In the old times when the roads were bad, and when it was more the custom to plough high lands than it is now, small horses were absolutely necessary to get over the ground. There was then very little demand for horses to carry on that large and growing class of town trade which is most successfully performed by the animal that can take the heaviest load.

Every year there is an increased demand in the rapidly-growing towns of Wales for the class of horse seen in railway waggons, warehouse vans, and brewers' drays in large English towns. Machynlleth fairs are attended from all parts of North Wales, because of their reputation for large horses of this class, and if a farmer has a heavy horse he wishes to sell he sends it to Machynlleth fair. The advantage in having heavy draught horses is that as a rule two of them will do nearly as much work as three of the lighter kind. A great deal of power is wasted in Wales by working three, four, and sometimes five horses in traces. Two horses in the shafts would do more work and accomplish it more satisfactorily. No small reform is more needed than for carts to be so constructed that two or three horses can be put in the shafts, so that their strength would tell on the load instead of being wasted. A load of coals, lime, or manure in a cart or waggon is drawn by one horse in the shafts and two or three in traces. A pair of horses in a carriage run side by side and share the work equally, but where the first object should be to utilize force just there we find force wasted by an arrangement apparently calculated to do the least amount of work at the greatest possible expenditure of labour. Rich men sometimes take pride in employing four horses to accomplish what one could do with ease, but poor farmers are certainly not so well off that they can afford to keep unnecessary horses, and yet that is just what the custom of a large portion of the country comes to. If an hotel keeper were to drive his omnibus to and from the railway station with a shaft horse and two tracers, there is not a farmer in the country who would not realize the absurd waste of power, but he cannot see that his four horses in a line with a load of lime or coal behind them are doing the very thing he would so quickly condemn if he found it in a town where he has been accustomed to see horses working abreast. The waste of power here noticed is partly due to the narrow bad roads, which are often so deeply rutted that two horses abreast would always be walking in the ruts, and partly to the carts which are so constructed that the load must rest upon the shaft horse.

CHAPTER XXII.

HORSES.—*(Continued.)*

MORE than once already reference has been made to the Welsh farmer's dread of increased rent; to his belief in the profitableness of bad farming; to his reluctance to pay his way in money; to his disregard of all manner of details, and to his unpunctuality. In writing about horses it is again necessary, even at the risk of being charged with repetition, to note the great difficulty there is in persuading farmers to pay, if needs be, a couple of guineas for the use of a horse with a long satisfactory pedigree, and whose stock commands a ready sale at high prices. Thirty shillings or two pounds expended on a sire may make a difference of forty or sixty guineas in the value of a colt, but still many farmers favour what they consider the cheapest horse, and thus entail upon themselves unnecessary and useless loss. The trouble and expense of rearing a foal worth £30 at three years old are as great as in rearing one worth double the money, and in addition there is far more difficulty in selling the £30 colt than in selling one worth £60 or £70. The demand in England for the better class of Welsh horses is almost unlimited; but the poorer sorts are a drug in the market.

Of course, farmers who only give five shillings for

the use of a horse take no care whatever of the mare while she is in foal, and leave the young colt very much to provide for itself; but when two guineas has been paid for a first-class stallion some regard is sure to be bestowed upon the mare, and the foal is worth a considerable amount as soon as it is thrown. Mares are frequently worked too hard when in foal, and at the best of times on poor farms horses only obtain the second best of the by no means superior accommodation afforded in average farm buildings. The good places are reserved for the cows, and the horses are left to take their chance. Cows kept in cold damp buildings do not give milk as freely as when housed in warm, dry, well-ventilated places. The reduced supply of milk is a form of loss the dullest of farmers quickly detects, and very likely provides against by sacrificing his horses. Horses stabled in draughty buildings, neither weather-proof nor clean, suffer in health and quickly deteriorate in value to an extent realized only by the more thoughtful agriculturist who knows too well that profits are impossible of attainment as long as he is compelled to pursue his business heavily weighted. A badly stabled horse may continue to do the work required by the farmer, but the results of neglect are discovered as soon as the animal is brought into the fair and offered for sale. This is one of those cases in which the farmer who tends his horse before he serves himself will feel that the statements are overdrawn, but it is only necessary to go up and down the country to see that a good deal needs to be done both by farmers and for them before live stock will be as profitable as it ought to be.

Many Welsh farmers treat young horses as severely as the Spartans treated their children, and on the same principle. The result is, perhaps, satisfactory in the case of the very strongest, but, as a rule, less rigorous training would be more profitable. Colts turned out until they are two years old and then set to work do not wear well. The strength of youth has been expended in combating adverse conditions of life, instead of in laying up a fund of strength for future use. These out-door trained horses, it is said, are not as firm on their legs or as sound in constitution as horses kept up and well fed during the first two years of life. Good food and shelter give to young horses a stability that enables them to wear well when subjected in after life to hard, continuous labour on the roads and in the fields. A good deal may be urged in favour of allowing horses to spend the first two years outside, but buyers prefer colts whose strength has not been subjected to this severe strain. The horse breeder may be willing to admit that colts have a better chance of developing into really useful animals if provided with good stables and plenty of food, but he may reasonably ask first for the stables and then for purchasers who will give increased prices for these horses. Purchasers may prefer a horse that has been kept up and yet may not be prepared to give the increased price that must be asked for him owing to the additional cost of his keep.

If it should be asserted that keeping young horses up would eventually advantage the buyer more than the seller, it must be admitted that the practice of selling colts at two years old is one that results in loss to the seller alone. A farmer who intends to make the greatest profit out of the horses he breeds keeps them until they are four years old instead of selling them at two as is common among poor farmers. At two years old a horse is only beginning to show what kind of an animal he may be, and the seller can then only obtain a very small share of the profit that would be his if he were prepared to wait until the animal was four years old, and had taken his permanent form. The difficulty a poor farmer experiences in keeping a colt after two years of age is great. He is pressed for money, and tempting offers are made to him that he is not in a position to resist. A horse sold by him for £35 or £40 he may hear has been sold for £100 or £120 in twelve months afterwards, but next year and next he will again be compelled to sell two-year-olds, equally promising, just because he has neither the accommodation nor the capital to enable him to keep them until their most profitable age. In horse breeding as in other departments of farming a good deal remains to be done, but there can be no question that in horses Wales has already learnt some valuable lessons, and is on the way to learn more. A much larger number of horses could easily be reared by small farmers with only a trifling additional cost to themselves. A mare is as useful as a gelding, as far as work is concerned, and will bring a valuable colt every year if care is taken in choosing a really good horse. The demand for horses, and especially for the strong, useful, fast trotting cobs of Wales, is growing with the increasing population, and if farmers were wise they would lay themselves out for this branch of business, which at any rate is more profitable than either wheat growing or store cattle rearing from mongrel bulls. What is required is that owners of large estates should join together and import first rate sires. If, however, landlords will not do this, they might see that tenants are supplied with properly constructed stables and cow-houses. No real saving it should be remembered can be effected by turning horses out of stables merely to accommodate milking cows. The loss arising from ruinous buildings may not be so quickly apparent in horses as in cows but it is quite as real.

Landowners cannot get rid of the responsibility that rests upon them by merely calling their tenants thriftless and void of enterprise. Want of thrift in tenants is as clear a proof of deficiencies among landlords as can be desired, and it is a simple matter of justice to tenant farmers in Wales to point out the great drawback they have to contend with in trying to carry on a difficult business under conditions unfavourable to success.

As regards the future, it is to be hoped that, either through agricultural societies or privately, landowners will offer prizes for entire horses sufficiently large to attract stallions from England and Scotland. If Welsh landowners took a pride in keeping entire horses, two stallion shows might be held annually, one for North and one for South Wales. Representatives from agricultural shows would attend these shows and engage horses to travel the districts, and in a short time instead of Wales having to go to England and Scotland for sires, those places would have to come to Wales. Hitherto, Welsh landlords have done so very little to improve the country that it is not unreasonable to expect them to take up horse breeding and make it their peculiar province. They could lose nothing, but might gain directly; indirectly they would certainly be profited. One reason for urging upon landlords the wisdom of taking up horse breeding is, that Wales already occupies a good position in this important branch, and might, with a little united action, take the lead. The defects and shortcomings pointed out are far from universal; in fact, Wales has more reason to be proud of her horses than of her horned cattle, her sheep, her white crops, or her roots. Horses are already a strong point, and with care might be made the pride of the country.

CHAPTER XXIII.

AGRICULTURAL EDUCATION.

FORMERLY a farmer who read books and tried experiments was looked upon as a deluded man on the road to certain ruin. If, however, as sometimes happened, instead of achieving ruin he made a fortune, his success was attributed to the excellence of his farm, a run of good luck, a series of favourable seasons, or to anything except the reading and the experiments. This objection to knowledge was not confined to farmers, and certainly not to farmers in Wales, who, as a class, are more intelligent and better read than their English brethren, and were amongst the very first to avail themselves of the facilities afforded by The Education Act (1870), for establishing elementary schools in rural districts. During the past ten or fifteen years a great deal has been said and written about education in Wales, and the actual progress made has not been inconsiderable when all the numerous drawbacks are taken into consideration.

The establishment of the University College of Wales at Aberystwyth is alone sufficient to mark an important epoch in the history of education. Hitherto, it is true, the College has not been supported by the wealthy landowners of the Principality, a fact which may be accounted for by the unfortunate action of the promoters and managers of the institution, but still good work may be done, especially for agriculture. The scheme, as at first formulated, it was afterwards found would not be carried out, and the College has ever since laboured under the depressing weight of a grandiloquent name, appropriate enough for the great undertaking originally suggested, but not at all suitable for the modest institution which finds a home in the magnificent pile of unfinished buildings at Aberyswyth.

The old prejudice against knowledge has died out to such an extent that the College Council felt justified some time ago in arranging for a series of lectures to be delivered to the students on the First Principles of Agriculture. These lectures, delivered by Professor Tanner, F.C.S., and subsequently published in a shilling volume, were open to schoolmasters, but, unfortunately, were not largely attended by them. Why the schoolmasters neglected an opportunity of this kind it is not easy to say, unless the management, as is so often the case, was at fault.

If in the Board and National Schools of Wales elementary agricultural knowledge was efficiently taught the effect would soon make itself felt in better farming, and in the practical recognition of those facts and principles which cannot without loss be ignored by the tiller of the soil, any more than by the merchant or the mechanic.

How strongly the Council of the University College feel the need for improved agricultural education in Wales, is shown by the creation of an Agricultural

Science department at Aberystwyth, notwithsanding the comparative failure of the former movement. This department has been established for the purpose of supplying, at moderate cost, a thoroughly good course of instruction in the sciences connected with agriculture, and the gentlemen who have been appointed to take charge of it are Professor Tanner, F.C.S., senior member of the Royal Agriculture College, examiner in agriculture, under the Government department of science, &c., and Professor Buckman, F.C.S., F.G.S., late Professor of natural history at the Royal Agricultural College. Judging from the measure of success that has attended the college up to the present time, 1878, it can scarcely be presumed that the scientific agricultural education the college is now capable of giving will be much sought after by the sons of the better class of farmers. However, something is gained by the publication of the fact that agricultural education is within the reach of Welshmen at a moderate cost. Part of the scheme is to establish in every county of Wales scholarships which are assisted by Government grants. If this new movement becomes as successful as its promoters anticipate, it will do more to raise the business of agriculture to its proper place in the estimation of the public than almost anything else that can be imagined.*

At present the farmer's business is held to be one followed only by those who are unable to make a living by less laborious and more profitable means.

---

*When the College re-opened in October last no agricultural students entered the College, and the new department has therefore not succeeded.

The Welsh farmer keenly feels that the social position he occupies is not equal to that occupied by Scotch and English agriculturists, but instead of trying to improve that position by elevating his calling, he leaves it and becomes a Dissenting Minister, a shopkeeper, or the owner of a London milk walk. Instead of its being the ambition of the owner of a London milk walk to secure a farm in Wales, it is the ambition of the farmer to secure a milk walk! Instruction in scientific agriculture can scarcely, of course, be expected to remedy all the evils that characterize the cultivation of land and the rearing of stock in the Principality. Those evils spring mainly from an utter disregard of punctuality, cleanliness, order, and attention to those details which ignorance everywhere tends to despise. Reform must be looked for chiefly in the direction of Board Schools, where agricultural labourers, it is to be hoped, in future will receive a training that will put in their proper place those principles which strike at the root of every business. There is no reason why the Welsh agricultural labourer should not be taught thoroughness in whatever he undertakes. Punctuality should be enforced as stringently as truthfulness, and order should be inculcated as regularly as honesty. It is the fashion just now to account for all sorts of defects and excellences by references to race, but the great corrector of national defects in the individual is severe training and strict discipline. The education that enables men to make the best of everything they are brought in contact with cannot have a wider or more fruitful field than in dealing with the growth of food, and the utilization of all natural products. The ignorant agricultural labourer or farmer lives in the presence of great waste, and is not even aware of the fact. Worse than that, he actually in his ignorance labours to bring about the very destruction he most wishes to avoid. There is scarcely an operation on the farm, whether in regard to stock or crops, in which knowledge he does not possess might not be used with profit.

That there is an education, so called, which unfits the farmer and labourer for their occupation and tends to fill them with contempt for their business is true; but that is no argument against the education which fits farmers for their business, and enables them to grapple successfully with all its complications. No great or sudden change can be expected in the nature of the instruction given to the children of the poor in agricultural districts, but the mere fact that this department of education is looked upon with favour at the University College of Wales, and deemed to be worthy of attention by those able to afford high class instruction, will have a beneficial effect upon the country. The good or ill effects of a tendency are not always recognized as clearly as they ought to be. If Welsh agriculturists can be persuaded that an ignorant farmer or labourer works under disadvantages which knowledge alone can remove, a great step in advance will have been made. Once let it be recognized that knowledge enables a man to bring about certain profitable results which are out of the reach of his more ignorant neighbour, and education will become a new force in the country. There may at first seem to be no connection between improved agricultural education and, say, the straggling broken fences which so clearly indicate the slovenly farmer; but let the advantage of good fences be realized, as perhaps they only can be realized, by men of some general culture, and the gaps will be repaired, gates will be procured, and hedges will be trimmed down. It is sometimes said that people, however poor they may be, could keep themselves clean. As a matter of fact, however, dirt is one of the most constant attendants upon poverty, just as disorder is the most regular attendant upon ignorance, although there is no reason why the ignorant should not be orderly. There can be no question that what is wanted is more education—not of the showy sort, but education that will reveal to the farmer and make plain to him the world of forces, adverse and beneficent, in which he lives—forces which he must control, or which will defeat all his efforts, and make him their slave.

CHAPTER XXIV.

SALES BY AUCTION.

THE business of the auctioneer in the rural districts of Wales is often adopted by farmers, broken down tradesmen, and others, who seldom entirely depend upon it for a living. In the larger towns auctioneers who understand their work succeed in obtaining support, but the farmer who has stock or crops to dispose of probably goes to the village auctioneer, saves £5 in commission, and in the end loses £50 or £100 in the amount realized. In the majority of instances the farmer has no confidence whatever in advertising, and the quack auctioneer is too ignorant to inspire him with confidence. It is not by any means an uncommon thing in country districts to see a rudely written notice announcing a sale, nailed to a gatepost at the entrance to a village, or fixed on the door of a blacksmith's shop. In addition to this primitive advertisement the bellman may be sent round the nearest market town once or twice to announce the forthcoming auction, but beyond the confines of the parish the sale is unknown. Printing has so far become the rule that written notices of sales are now the exception, except in remote districts. Bills, however, are often very small, and are confined only to the narrow district where, in

L

all probability, news of the sale would be obtained without any public announcement at all. Newspapers, however widely circulated, are not recognised by the inhabitants of rural districts as a cheap, efficient means of announcing sales of stock and crops amongst butchers, dealers, and others who are most likely to become buyers, and who think very little of travelling thirty or forty miles to a good sale. To pay thirty shillings for an advertisement in a newspaper appears to the farmer to be an act of gross waste for which no excuse or sufficient justification can be made. He may lose far more than that amount in the price realised for one cow, or horse, but there is always the doubt whether after all a sale widely announced would have been more successful, and the saving in expenses is certain. Besides, the opponent of wide publicity can always refer to one or more of his neighbours who employed a first class auctioneer to conduct the sale, and spent a considerable sum in bills and newspaper advertisements, and who did not realize much more money than the quack auctioneer who was only paid ten or fifteen shillings for the job, and whose bill for advertising was more than covered by five shillings.

Good auctioneers who suffer from the competition of quacks, would be well pleased if the Chancellor of the Exchequer decided to double or treble the price of the licence which now costs £10, a sum not likely to deter any man if he can only obtain one sale to start with. The rule is for a man who sets up as auctioneer not to take out his licence until he has made sure of at least one sale. If the law compelled auctioneers to renew their licences at a certain time, and to pay the full amount for any portion of a year, the auctioneer's business would be purged of many hangers on, who are always ready to take out a licence or to leave it alone as suits them best. In a thickly populated country the evil consequences of this kind of competition would scarcely be felt by the regular professional man, but in Wales, every competitor who ekes out a living by shop-keeping, farming, beer-shop keeping, and other occupations in addition to auctioneering, helps to lower the business of the auctioneer below the level it ought to occupy for the security of farmers and others.

Men who fail in the businesses they were trained to are, thanks to School Boards and Government Inspection, no longer able to earn a living as schoolmasters; consequently many of them start as auctioneers, not because they understand the value of all kinds of property, but because they imagine no special training, or knowledge, or power is required by an auctioneer. A greater mistake could not be made, as many a poor Welsh farmer knows to his great cost. If his love of quacks sends the farmer to an amateur doctor he may fortunately lose his life and so be unable to realize how his confidence has been abused, but if he goes to a quack auctioneer he simply loses money, and is therefore able to understand and appreciate the unpleasant consequences of his mistake and to moan over it.

In England, and in a few places on the Welsh border, monthly, fortnightly, or weekly sales of stock by auction have superseded the old annual or half-yearly cattle fairs. In the Principality, and particularly in the more thinly populated portions of it, these sales have been tried and in many cases have failed. Sometimes the monthly fair has become a qualified success, but the sales of stock by auction are a step so far in advance of old customs that the farmer cannot bring himself to trust them. The method he is most in favour of is to sit at home until a butcher or jobber comes round and bargains with him over a pipe and perhaps a glass of cwrw slowly and patiently hour after hour. That is a course he can understand. But to drive his cattle or sheep into the market town on the monthly or weekly fair day, to hand them over to an auctioneer to be numbered, to see them walked out one by one and sold under his eyes in a few minutes; these are things that give rise in his mind to a sense of insecurity and change that is far from pleasing or soothing to his self love. If he must come to the fair he will stand with his stock and chaffer and haggle about half-a-crown, delighted with the consciousness that the more difficult the bargain, the more certain he may be that the price obtained is a good one ; and, most important consideration, he has not paid the auctioneer a commission!

That good markets, monthly or fortnightly fairs and sales of stock by auction are to the advantage of farmers may be proved, if proof is necessary, by the fact that butchers and dealers in small places are opposed to them as strongly as the small retail tradesman is opposed to the co-operative store. The large dealer cannot afford to spend half a day in purchasing a cow or half-a-dozen sheep, and therefore he leaves the higgling part to men who know perfectly well when they are buying that they are only middle men, and that the prices they can give are not as high as will be given by the large dealers, to whom they intend to sell again. The sale by auction, by merely introducing the ready-money system, confers a great benefit, which farmers who have lost money by selling on credit will be able to estimate for themselves. The practice of giving long credit, which does so much to hinder progress in every kind of business in Wales, is largely practised in sales by auction. "Six months' credit will be given, subject to conditions," is a common feature in notices of sales by auction. It is very doubtful whether this credit system pays the seller, who should never forget that although the credit may bring together a number of questionable buyers, it always keeps away the best sort. The credit may be of advantage to local men, but the "foreign" buyer who ought always to be sought after wants no credit, and carefully avoids sales by auction where it is given.

There is no department of his business where the farmer is more completely dependent upon the honesty and integrity of the persons he deals with than when he sells his produce by auction. An honest, straightforward auctioneer who does not favour friends and who never buys for himself unless he tells the company after he has got all the bids he can that he will give more than they have offered, is worth all he costs. He should be a man of some substance, and one who has a character and a reputation to lose. Some sort of an auctioneer may always be obtained at a low price. but like most low-priced articles, he is liable to prove in unpleasant ways that he was dear at the money. The fairest way to pay auctioneers is by commission, and that is the way they prefer to be paid, but the desire is great among the poorer sort of farmers to induce the salesman to accept a fixed sum instead of commission. By this means the auctioneer is liable to be underpaid, and in addition has taken away from him one powerful incentive to obtain the highest possible prices. There is an impression in the minds of farmers that a really first class auctioneer is not willing to take small sales. This is a mistake. There is perhaps not an auctioneer in Wales, however large his business, who does not take a small sale and conduct it as well as if the value of property to be disposed of amounted to thousands.

MORGAN & THORPE,

General Agents and Accountants,

AGENTS FOR

MESSRS. BRADBURY & CO.,
LIVERPOOL:

BRADBURY'S CELEBRATED CONCENTRATED CATTLE FOOD, a truly valuable article for Feeding and Fattening Cattle, Sheep, Pigs, &c.

BRADBURY'S CELEBRATED BUTTER POWDER, invaluable to all Dairy Farmers for increasing the quantity and improving the quality of Butter.

BRADBURY'S SHEEP DIPPING POWDER, the Best and Safest Sheep Dip in the world.

BRADBURY'S CELEBRATED FLY POWDER, the most certain, safe, and effectual preparation for preventing the Fly striking Sheep and Lambs, and destroying the Maggot.

AGENTS FOR

MESSRS. E. & W. PEARSON,
LIVERPOOL,
LINSEED AND OIL CAKE MANUFACTURERS.

AGENTS FOR

MESSRS. ALEXANDER M. SMITH & CO.,
MANUFACTURERS OF THE

Celebrated Palm Nut Meal, Palm Nut Cake, and Cocoa Nut Cake.

AGENTS FOR

The Guardian Horse and Vehicle Assurance Association (Limited).

Also, Agents for all kinds of Manures, Seeds, &c.

For enquiries respecting orders, and for general information, apply to

MORGAN & THORPE,
GENERAL AGENTS AND ACCOUNTANTS,
CARDIGAN HOUSE, QUEEN'S ROAD, ABERYSTWYTH.

SPOONER & Co.,
PORTMADOC.

FOUR-WHEEL COUPLED TANK LOCOMOTIVE

FOR

Quarries, Mines, Wharves, and Tram Roads.

Made in Sizes from $1\frac{1}{2}$ to 12 tons.

These engines will take respectively loads from 40 to 800 tons at an average speed of 8 miles an hour.

By the adoption of a 2-ton engine a saving of £60 per annum can be effected for every two horses previously used.

For further particulars and prices apply to

SPOONER & Co.,
PORTMADOC.

SPOONER & Co.,
PORTMADOC.

THE PATENT "ROBEY" FIXED ENGINE,
Which for simplicity of design, ease of erection, economy in first cost and in working, is unapproached by any other engine.

Very slight foundations are required and no brick chimney, thus saving great cost in brick-work, being a

GREAT SAVING OF TIME AND EXPENSE IN FIXING.
CAN BE SEEN AT WORK ON APPLICATION.
For reduced prices and further particulars apply to the
SOLE MANUFACTURERS,
ROBEY & Co., Engineers,
LINCOLN.

Or to

SPOONER & Co., Engineers,
PORTMADOC,

Who in the event of your requiring steam power, will be happy to call upon you and discuss the matter.

(In sizes from 4 to 200 horse-power always in stock or in progress.)
(Are now extensively used for driving Saw Mills, Flour Mills, Brickmaking Machinery and Factories, and for winding and pumping in Quarries and Mines.)

Old Established Nursery, Seed, & Implement Business, Chester.

JAMES DICKSON & SONS,
108, EASTGATE STREET,
AND
"NEWTON" NURSERIES,
CHESTER.
ALSO,
CORN EXCHANGE IMPLEMENT WAREHOUSE, CHESTER.

Priced Catalogues and particulars as to Free Delivery, &c., Post Free.

The Nursery Stock is VERY EXTENSIVE, of UNEXCEPTIONAL QUALITY, and comprises the following in GREAT variety:—

FOREST TREES.	**FRUIT TREES.**
COVERT PLANTS.	**EVERGREENS.**
HEDGE PLANTS.	**ROSES.**
CONIFERS.	**AMERICAN PLANTS**
VINES.	**STOVE PLANTS.**
GREENHOUSE PLANTS.	**BEDDING PLANTS.**

ORNAMENTAL FOLIAGE, and other Trees and Plants, &c., &c.

The SEED DEPARTMENT has the most careful attention possible, therefore Seeds of the MOST RELIABLE description for the VARIOUS SEASONS can at all times be supplied:—

FOR SPRIN.	FOR AUTUMN.
DICKSON'S SELECT PRIZE SWEDE and TURNIP of all sorts.	TURNIP of sorts.
DICKSON'S DEFIANCE YELLOW GLOBE and MANGEL WURZEL of all sorts.	SCARLET CLOVER.
	MUSTARD.
	WINTER VETCHES.
CARROT. all sorts.	,, RAPE.
GRASSES, ,,	,, OATS.
CLOVERS, ,,	,, RYE.
MIXTURES for PERMANENT PASTURE and MEADOW, for Renovating OLD PASTURES, for LAWNS, PARKS, &c.	RENOVATING MIXTURE.
	PERMANENT PASTURE MIXTURES.
	LAWN MIXTURE.
VEGETABLE SEEDS.	OX CABBAGE:
FLOWER SEEDS: and all others for Farm and Garden.	and all other Seeds for Farm and Garden.

The AGRICULTURAL IMPLEMENT AND MACHINE DEPARTMENT offers every advantage to intending purchasers, and the opportunity for selection at the CORN EXCHANGE IMPLEMENT WAREHOUSE is in every way superior.

BRANCH NURSERIES:—
Newtown, Montgomeryshire ; & Dolgelley, Merionethshire.

E. PURSER & Co.,

(LONDON MANURE Co.,)

ESTABLISHED 1840,

Have now Ready for Delivery in Dry fine condition,

PURSER'S PURE DISSOLVED BONES,
BONE MANURE,
SUPERPHOSPHATE,
BONE TURNIP MANURE,
PURSER'S CHEMICALLY TREATED GUANO,
NITROPHOSPHATE,
URATE,
CORN, MANGOLD, & POTATO MANURES.

Offices—116, *FENCHURCH STREET, E.C.*

Storekeeper at Carmarthen—JOHN LLOYD, 12, Nott Square.
Do. *Newport*—GEORGE TREW, Monmouthshire Railway Wharf.

For the convenience of Customers in North and South Wales, the London Manure Company have established Depôts at Newport, Mon., Aberdovey, Carmarthen, and Saltney, and the above Manures can be obtained by applying to their regular Agents in all the principal Towns in North and South Wales.

JOHN FOWLER & Co.,
STEAM PLOUGH WORKS, LEEDS.
LONDON OFFICES—71, CORNHILL, E.C.

MANUFACTURERS OF PATENT

STEAM PLOUGHING
AND CULTIVATING MACHINERY,
SUITABLE FOR ALL COUNTRIES AND EVERY DESCRIPTION OF SOIL.

SPECIAL IMPLEMENTS are made to suit the cultivation of SUGAR CANES, BEET ROOT, and every other Crop, and also for the RECLAMATION of WASTE LAND. A set of Machinery can be seen in operation near the Works, at Leeds (distant about 4 hours from London), at any time by giving a few days' notice.

TRACTION ENGINES
For hauling HEAVY LOADS, and suitable for ALL AGRICULTURAL PURPOSES.
LOCOMOTIVE ENGINES & MACHINERY
For Colliery and Mining Purposes.

Including SINKING, WINDING, and PUMPING ENGINES, AIR COMPRESSORS, and Patent CLIP PULLEYS for Inclines, &c., &c.

Also Decauville's Patent Portable Tramway.

Descriptive Catalogues, with Prices, free on application.

THE CHAMPION PLOUGH
OF ENGLAND.

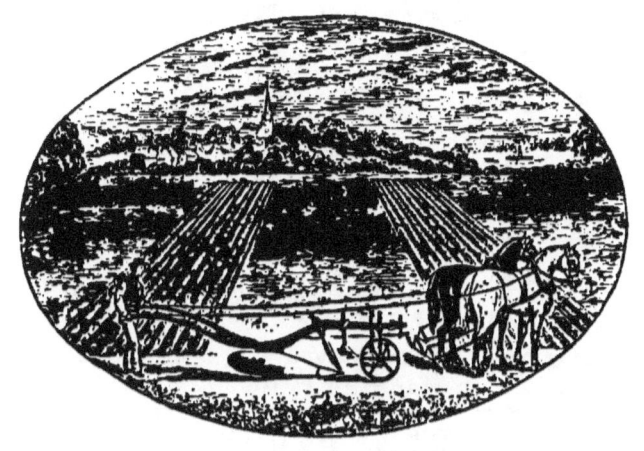

J. & F. HOWARD,

Britannia Iron Works, Bedford, England,

MANUFACTURERS OF

Ploughs,	Haymakers.
Harrows,	Mowers,
Horse Rakes,	Reapers,

AND

STEAM PLOUGHING MACHINERY.

Illustrated Catalogues Post Free.

M. and G. have ready for delivery

PURE GROUND BONES,

Containing 55 %. Phosphates and 4 %. Ammonia, at lowest market prices.

GENUINE RAW PERUVIAN GUANO,

Free from Stones, and standard of Phosphates and Ammonia certified.

M. & G. have made special arrangements with the Government Agents, enabling them to offer at same prices, either in small or large quantities, as if purchased at the Depôts.

SOLUBLE PERUVIAN GUANO

In beautiful dry and fine condition. Analysis guaranteed.

WHEAT, BEAN, AND BLOOD MANURES; DISSOLVED BONES AND SUPERPHOSPHATES.

MORRIS & GRIFFIN,

Ceres Works, Wolverhampton.

MR. GEO. BRUNTON,
ESTATE AGENT,
GROES COTTAGE,
Near WELSHPOOL.
MONTGOMERYSHIRE.

THE LEADING NEWSPAPER
For a great District in Wales, including
CARDIGANSHIRE, MERIONETHSHIRE, & SOUTH CARNARVONSHIRE.

THE

CAMBRIAN NEWS,
MERIONETHSHIRE STANDARD,
AND ABERYSTWYTH TIMES.
EVERY FRIDAY MORNING. PRICE 1½d.

SOLD BY AGENTS IN
Aberystwith, Aberaeron, Aberdovey, Bala, Bangor, Barmouth, Bettws-y-Coed, Borth, Cardigan, Carmarthen, Carnarvon, Chester, Corwen, Criccieth, Dinas Mawddwy, Dolgelley, Festiniog, Harlech, Lampeter, Liverpool, Llanidloes, Llanilar, London, Machynlleth, Manchester, Newtown, Penrhyndeudraeth, Portmadoc, Pwllheli, Towyn, Tregaron, Welshpool, &c., &c., &c.

THE CAMBRIAN NEWS AND ABERYSTWYTH TIMES
HAS NOW BEEN

𝔈stablished between 19 and 20 Years,

And has no rival in influence and circulation in the greater part of the District, which includes the important Seaports, Watering Places, and Trading Districts, mentioned above, the news of which it reports and discusses.

The Cambrian News and Aberystwyth Times also deals with General Questions affecting the Principality, and contains occasional Welsh Contributions; also Bye-Gones, Local Sketches, &c.

Published by JACOB JONES, Bala; D. LLOYD, Portmadoc; and at Aberystwyth, by J. GIBSON, at the Office, 3, Queen's Road.

PATENT   CHAIN HARROW

FIRST PRIZE   FIRST PRIZE

IMPLEMENTS   IN EVERY COMPETITI

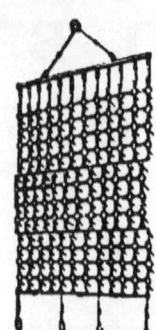

LATE
CAMBRIDGE & CO.,

Portable Engines	Disintegrators
Vertical Engines	Bone Mills
Horizontal Engines	Patent Corn Mil
Horse Gears	Sack Lifts
"Cambridge" Rolls	Hydraulic Lifts
"Cambridge" Notch Rolls	Tanks, Painted
	,, Galvani
"Cambridge" Patent Harrows	Boilers, Cornish
	,, Portabl
Excelsior Harrows	,, Vertical
Drag Harrows	
Scufflers	
&c., &c.	

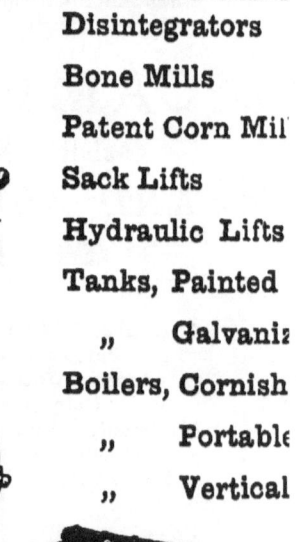

APPLY FOR COMPLETE CATALOGUE.

ST. PHILIP'S IRON WORK

WOODALL AND VENABLES'S PUBLICATIONS.

History of the Gwydir Family, with notes from the Brogyntyn, Wynnstay, and Peniarth MSS. never before published. Illustrated with Portraits, &c. On thick, hand-made paper, in large type, bound in cloth, bevelled boards, £1 1s.

Gossiping Guide to Wales. 1s. 6d. Popular Edition, Five Maps, 176 pp. 2s. 6d. Half-Crown Edition, Cloth, Five Maps, Routes, and Panorama from Snowdon (3 feet long, containing 150 points seen from the summit), specially drawn for the work. 5s. Crown Edition, Cloth Gilt, 12 Maps, Routes, Geological and Botanical Chapters, and *Coloured* Snowdon Panorama. 246 pp.

"A model in its way."—*Daily News.*
"By far the most amusing guide we have seen."—*Standard.*
"One of the most perfect productions of its kind ever issued."—*South Wales Daily News.*
"Sure to become a favourite with the multitude."—*The Field.*
"Not only a trusty guide, but a most genial companion."—*Liverpool Daily Post.*

Wynnstay and the Wynns, a Volume of Varieties, put together by the author of "The Gossiping Guide to Wales." Dedicated by permission to Lady Williams Wynn. With 12 Illustrations—Portraits, Views of Wynnstay, Llangedwyn, &c. Bound in Green Cloth Gilt, red edges, 5s.; Red Cloth Gilt, bevelled boards, gilt edges, and printed on superior paper, 7s. 6d. Sent free by Post.

The Book of the Choir, a Manual for Choristers.
"Should be in every Chorister's hand."—*Bookseller.*
"We can speak with entire approval of this small but complete manual."—*Church Review.*

The Railway Record, Monthly, 1d., with Time Tables of North and Mid-Wales and Shropshire, connections with the great English towns, &c.

The Oswestry Advertizer, Wednesday, Price 1½d., a Newspaper circulating in Shropshire, Montgomeryshire, Denbighshire, and other counties. Established 30 years. The best medium for Advertising in a large District.

PRINTING, LITHOGRAPHING,
BINDING, PUBLISHING, &c.

At the Caxton Works, Oswestry, which are fitted up with a large number of Presses and Steam-Driven Machines for Printing and Lithographing, Ruling, Cutting, Binding, Perforating, Numbering, &c., WOODALL AND VENABLES are prepared to execute all kinds of work in the above-named branches with expedition and at moderate prices.

Books, Pamphlets, Sermons, Magazines, &c., Published.

Lithographed Plans, Autograph Circulars, Bills of Quantities, Letter Headings, Invoice and Account Headings, &c.

WOODALL AND VENABLES beg to inform Solicitors, Accountants, and Men of Business, who require small or large numbers of Circulars, Applications for Accounts, Prices Current, &c., expeditiously printed, that they will supply at 2s. 6d. per bottle a Lithographic Writing Ink, by which the original can be written on ordinary paper with an ordinary pen in their own offices, and then forwarded to the Caxton Works, where it will be lithographed in facsimile, and the quantity required sent by return of post.

CAXTON WORKS, OSWESTRY.

ARDWYN SCHOOL,
ABERYSTWYTH.

Head Master: The Rev. LLEWELYN EDWARDS, M.A.,

Of Lincoln College, Oxford, and Graduate in Classical Honours.

THE situation of Ardwyn is recognised as the most delightful and salubrious near the town of Aberystwyth; it is within view of the sea and well sheltered from the northerly and easterly winds. The House (expressly planned by a London Architect) is surrounded by three acres of ground laid out for Croquet, Play-ground, &c. For Cricket and Football the boys have the use of a field not far from the House.

Mr. Edwards prepares his pupils specially for Matriculation at the Universities, for the Scholarship Examination at the University College of Wales, for the Oxford and Cambridge Local Examinations, for the Medical and Law Preliminary Examinations, as well as for Commercial Pursuits.

There are Scholarships belonging to the School.

Terms:—For Boarders, from 40 to 45 Guineas per annum; Day Scholars, from 6 to 8 Guineas per annum

www.ingramcontent.com/pod-product-compliance
Lightning Source LLC
Chambersburg PA
CBHW030254170426
43202CB00009B/742